hugo

T0332140

PORTUGUESE
IN 3 MONTHS

Maria Fernanda Allen

YOUR ESSENTIAL GUIDE TO UNDERSTANDING AND SPEAKING PORTUGUESE

FREE AUDIO APP

THIRD EDITION
Series Editor Elise Bradbury
Senior Editor Amelia Petersen
US Editor Heather Wilcox
Senior Art Editor Jane Ewart
Managing Editors Christine Stroyan, Carine Tracanelli
Managing Art Editor Anna Hall
Production Editor Robert Dunn
Senior Production Controller Samantha Cross
Jacket Project Art Editor Surabhi Wadhwa-Gandhi
Jacket Design Development Manager Sophia MTT
Art Director Karen Self
Associate Publishing Director Liz Wheeler
Publishing Director Jonathan Metcalf

DK INDIA
Project Art Editor Anjali Sachar
Senior DTP Designer Shanker Prasad
Managing Editor Rohan Sinha
Managing Art Editor Sudakshina Basu

This American Edition, 2022
First American Edition, 1997
Published in the United States by DK Publishing,
a division of Penguin Random House LLC
1745 Broadway, 20th Floor, New York, NY 10019
First published in Great Britain by
Hugo's Language Books Limited

Copyright © 1997, 2003, 2022 Dorling Kindersley Limited
24 25 10 9 8 7 6 5
005–326925–Jan/2022

Written by Maria Fernanda Allen
Former lecturer in Portuguese at The University of Westminster,
London (Post-Graduate Dept. and other courses)
and a Fellow of the Institute of Linguists

A catalog record for this book is available from the Library of Congress.
ISBN 978-0-7440-5163-6

DK books are available at special discounts when purchased in bulk for sales
promotions, premiums, fund-raising, or educational use. For details contact:
DK Publishing Special Markets, 1745 Broadway, 20th Floor, New York, NY 10019
Special Sales@dk.com

Printed and bound in China

www.dk.com

This book was made with Forest
Stewardship Council™ certified
paper – one small step in DK's
commitment to a sustainable future.
Learn more at
www.dk.com/uk/information/sustainability

Preface

This edition of *Hugo Portuguese in 3 Months* was written by Maria Fernanda Allen, whose experience in teaching her native tongue ranges from beginners to post-graduate level. The course is designed for people learning at home who want to acquire a good working knowledge of Portuguese in a short time. The grammar is presented concisely and clearly, maintaining the Hugo principle of teaching only what is really essential and yet providing a complete introduction to written and conversational Portuguese.

The course is designed to teach the language as it is spoken in Portugal, but common variations between this and Brazilian Portuguese are noted in the book. It begins with an explanation of Portuguese pronunciation, as far as this is possible in print. We strongly encourage you to download the free *DK Hugo in 3 Months* app (see p.4) and to listen to the accompanying audio as you work through the course—this will enable you to learn the distinctive sounds of the Portuguese language. Referring to our system of "imitated pronunciation" in the initial weeks of the course will also help.

The grammar is presented in a practical way, in an order designed for the learner to make rapid progress. Constructions are clearly explained, and the exercises are designed to consolidate what you've learned. The conversations reinforce the points that have been seen as well as introduce idioms and colloquialisms for a thorough grasp of everyday Portuguese.

Ideally, you should try to spend about an hour a day on the course, although there is no hard and fast rule on this. Do as much as you feel capable of doing; it's much better to learn a little at a time, and to learn that thoroughly.

Before beginning a new section, always spend ten minutes reviewing what you learned the day before. Then, read each new section carefully, ensuring that you have fully understood the grammar, before listening to the audio to learn the pronunciation of sample sentences and new vocabulary. Finally, complete the exercises that accompany each section. Repeat them until the answers come easily. With the conversations, we suggest that you listen to them first and then read them aloud to see how closely you can imitate the voices on the recording. Repetition is vital to language learning. The more often you listen to a conversation or repeat an oral exercise, the faster your listening skills and fluency in speaking will improve.

The course is ends with a list of useful expressions. These will add to your comprehension, widen your vocabulary, and will be useful if you decide to take your study of Portuguese to a more advanced level.

When you've completed the course, you should have a very good understanding of the language—more than sufficient for general holiday or business purposes, and enough to lead to language validation tests if this is your eventual aim. We hope you enjoy *Hugo Portuguese in 3 Months* and wish you success with your studies!

About the audio app

The audio app that accompanies this Portuguese course contains audio recordings for all numbered sections, vocabulary boxes, conversations, and many of the exercises. There is no audio for Weeks 11 and 12. All audio is European Portuguese.

◀× Where you see this symbol, it indicates that there is no audio for that section.

To start using the audio with this book, go to **www.dk.com/hugo** and download the *DK Hugo In 3 Months* app on your smartphone or tablet from the App Store or Google Play. Then, select Portuguese from the list of titles.

Please note that this app is not a stand-alone course. It is designed to be used together with the book to familiarize you with Portuguese speech and to provide examples for you to repeat aloud.

Contents

Pronunciation

STRESS

Before starting to learn the sounds of Portuguese vowels and consonants, it is essential to learn a few rules about stress. Words are made up of syllables—groups of two or three letters, which must include a vowel. In both English and Portuguese, some of these syllables are stressed, and some are unstressed. In English, the stress is variable. For example, the first syllable is stressed in "ENG-land," while the stress falls on the second syllable in "gir-AFFE." In Portuguese, there are certain rules about which syllable is stressed.

A Portuguese word is normally stressed on the second-to-last syllable. For example, **marmelada**, which has four syllables (**mar-me-la-da**), is stressed on the penultimate **la**. The exceptions to this rule are:

- if the word has an accent on a vowel, in which case the accented syllable is stressed.
- if the word ends in an **l**, **r**, **z**, or **i**, in which case the last syllable is stressed.
- if the word ends in a diphthong or nasal vowel (see pp.11–12), in which case the last syllable is stressed.

As in English, the sound of letters may vary depending on whether they are stressed. So, in **marmelada**, the stressed **a** is pronounced [ah], while the unstressed **a**'s are pronounced [uh].

Accent marks you will see in Portuguese are the acute (´), the grave (`), the tilde (~), and the circumflex (^).

PRONUNCIATION

The following tips on pronouncing the vowels and consonants in Portuguese should help you master the most elusive as well as the most obvious sounds.

Naturally, the best way to perfect your pronunciation is to practice with the audio available on the app that accompanies this course. At the end of each subsection, as another aid to learning, you can sound out the phonetic transcriptions in the "imitated pronunciation" provided in the first few weeks of the course.

When reading the imitated pronunciation, avoid pauses between the syllables. Pronounce them as if they formed part of an English word, putting the stress on the syllable with a stress mark (') before it. Italicized letters are barely sounded.

The Portuguese have an irrepressible tendency to link the sound of a terminal (or final) vowel with the beginning of the next word; this liaison results in **ele era** sounding like el-'leh-ruh, or **nove horas** ('noh'veh and 'oh-rush) becoming noh-'voh-rush.

THE PORTUGUESE ALPHABET

A	(ah)	**N**	(enn*e*)
B	(bay)	**O**	(oh)
C	(say)	**P**	(pay)
D	(day)	**Q**	(kay)
E	(eh)	**R**	(err*e*)
F	(eff*e*)	**S**	(ess*e*)
G	(zhay*)	**T**	(tay)
H	('ah-gah)	**U**	(oo)
I	(ee)	**V**	(vay)
J	(zhah-tuh*)	**X**	(sheesh)
L	(ell*e*)	**Z**	(zay)
M	(emm*e*)		

The letters **K** ['kah-puh], **W** ['doo-ble vay], and **Y** [ee-'gray-goo] are not in use today, except in foreign words.

*The letters "zh" in the imitated pronunciation represent the sound of the s in the English word "measure."

VOWELS

a   This is an open vowel, like the long "ah" in "father," in a stressed syllable, before a final **l** or **r** , and when it has an acute or grave accent. Otherwise, it is like the short "uh" sound in "a̲bout."
For example:
camada [kuh-'mah-duh] layer
falar [fuh-'lahr] to speak
animal [uh-nee-'mahl] animal
chá [shah] tea

It becomes nasal when it has a tilde (**ã**); the italic *n* we use to indicate this sound should not be pronounced as a proper n, but more like the end of "sing," without strongly vocalizing the g.
For example:
irmã ['eer-ma*n*] sister

When the **a** has a circumflex accent (**â**), the sound is unchanged, but this syllable is stressed instead of the usual second-to-last syllable.
For example:
alfândega [al-'fahn-d*e*-guh] customs

e   This is an open vowel sound (as in "vet") in a stressed syllable, before **l**, and with grave or acute accents. Unstressed, it is barely voiced, which we indicate with an italicized *e*. In Brazil, however, the unstressed **e** is pronounced like the double "ee" in "see." For example:
metro ['meh-troo] meter, metro
café [kuh-'feh] coffee
mel [mehl] honey
secretária (s*e*-kr*e*-'tah-ree-uh) secretary

The closed vowel **e** is pronounced similarly to "ay" in "they." It occurs in some stressed syllables, when it has a circumflex accent (**ê**), and before a final **r**.
For example:
pelo ['pay-loo] fur
comer [koo-'mayr] to eat
vê [vay] he/she sees

When an **e** is by itself or forms the first syllable on its own, it is pronounced like the "ee" in "see."
For example:
edifício [ee-dee-'fee-sy'oo] building

i This is always pronounced "ee," but when unstressed, it should be given a slightly shorter sound. For example:
parti [par-'tee] I left

o If it is stressed, has an acute accent, or comes before **l**, the **o** is an open vowel sound similar to the "aw" sound in "rock." For example:
avó [uh-'vo] grandmother
sol [sol] sun
morte ['mor'te] death

It has a closed vowel sound similar to the long o in "no" in some stressed syllables, before a final **r**, and with the circumflex accent. This is the most common sound for **o** in Brazil. For example:
avô [uh-'voh] grandfather
amor [uh-'mohr] love
folha ['foh-l'yuh] leaf

It has the sound of "oo" in unstressed syllables and when it is on its own. For example:
tomar [too-'mahr] to take
gato ['gah-too] cat

When it has a tilde (**õ**) or precedes an **n**, it has a nasal sound, which we transcribe in the same way as explained under **ã**. See also the section on nasal vowels and diphthongs.

u This is always pronounced "oo": For example:
rua [roo'uh] street

DIPHTHONGS: VOWEL COMBINATIONS

When two vowels are pronounced as one syllable, this is called
a diphthong. Examples of diphthongs in English are "coin" or
"loud." In Portuguese, there are various vowel combinations that
are pronounced as diphthongs, notably:

ai	=	ah'ee as in "my"	**vai** ['vah'ee] he/she/it goes
au	=	ah'oo	**mau** ['mah'oo] bad
ao	=	ah'oh	**ao** ['ah'oh] at the, to the
ei	=	ay as in "tame"	**falei** [fuh-'lay'ee] I spoke
eu	=	ay'oo	**meu** [may'oo] my
oi	=	oy'e	**foi** [foy'e] he/she/it went
ou	=	o	**falou** [fuh-'lo] he/she spoke
ui	=	oo'e	**fui** [foo'e] I went

Although the transcriptions are indicated as syllables, note that
these vowel combinations blend together to form a single
sound. Run the sounds together as if you were speaking quickly.

Note: When there is an accent over one of two vowels
appearing together, you should treat the two vowels separately,
not as a diphthong: **seu** is a diphthong, but **céu** ['say-oo] is not.

NASAL VOWELS AND DIPHTHONGS

Whenever the vowels **a**, **e**, **i**, **o**, and **u** precede **m** and **n** or
have a tilde accent (**õ**), they become nasal. If you speak any
French, you should be familiar with the sound—for example, in
vin or *mon*. The closest approximation in English is the nasalized
sound in words ending in -ng, such as "sing" or "wrong," but
note that the -ng is barely pronounced. We indicate this in the
transcriptions with an *n* in italics.

The nasal diphthongs **ão**, **ãe**, **ãi**, and **õe** similarly need to be
sounded through your nose in this way. For example:
encanto [e*n*-'kahn-too] charm
jardim [zhar-'dee*n*] garden
ontem ['o*n*-te*n*] yesterday
untar [oo*n*-'tahr] to grease
não [nah'oo*n*] no
limões [lee-'maw'i*n*sh] lemons

CONSONANTS

These are pronounced as in English, with these exceptions:

c   This sounds like s in "silver" when it comes before **e** or **i**, or like the hard c in "cat" before **a**, **o**, and **u**, unless it has a cedilla (**ç**), which changes the sound to s. The combination **ch** is pronounced like an English "sh." For example:
cinema [see-'nay-muh] cinema
comer [koo-'mayr] to eat
começar [koo-m*e*-'sahr] to begin
chave ['shah-v*e*] key

d   In Portugal, the **d** sounds almost like "th" in "though." In Brazil, it is a harder sound, almost like in English.

g   Sounds like the "zh" sound of the s in "treasure" when coming before **e** or **i**. For example:
geral [zhuh-'rahl] general
gigante [zhee-'gah*n*-t*e*] giant

It is hard, as in "get," before **a**, **o**, **u**, and preceding a consonant. For example:
gordo ['gohr-doo] fat

When in the combination **gu**, before **e** or **i**, the **u** is not pronounced—it is only there to ensure a hard **g**.
For example:
guerra ['gehr-ruh] war
guitarra [gee-'tahr-ruh] guitar

h   This is never pronounced.

j   Sounds like the "zh" sound in "treasure." It precedes **a**, **o**, **u**, but hardly ever **e**. For example:
jardim [zhar-'dee*n*] garden
joia ['zhoh-yuh] jewel

l   The final **l** is pronounced strongly in Portugal, but in Brazil it has a faint quality. For example:
fácil ['fah-seel] easy [in Brazil: 'fah-see'oo]

lh   Give this a liquid sound, like the "ly-" in "billiards."
For example:
melhor [me-'l'yohr] better
milho ['mee-l'yoo] maize

nh   Pronounced like the the "ny-" in "onion." For example:
minha ['mee-n'yuh] mine

qu   Has a hard k sound as in "kit." The **u** that follows it is not pronounced before **e** or **i**. For example:
qual [kwal] which
quem [ken] who

r   Has a soft sound, close to the Italian r, when between vowels. It is more strongly rolled, like the Scottish or Spanish r, when it is doubled or comes at the beginning of a word. At the end of a word or syllable, it is emphasized even more. But in Brazil, the final **r** is usually not sounded. For example:
barato [buh-'rah-too] cheap
carro ['kah-rroo] car
amor [uh-'mohr] love

s   Is like the s in "salt" when beginning a word, doubled, or after a consonant. Between vowels, it is less sibilant, like s in "rose" or z in "zebra." In Portugal, the final **s** of a word or syllable sounds like "sh" in "sheep," although Brazilians sound a final **s** more like we do in English. For example:
sonho ['so-n'yoo] dream
rosa ['roh-zuh] rose
lápis ['lah-peesh] pencil

cesto ['say-shtoo] basket
When a word with a final **s** is followed by a word beginning with a vowel, the **s** is pronounced like z, not as "sh."

t   In Portugal, this is always pronounced as in "tea." In Brazil, it sounds more like "ch"—especially before **e** and **i**.

x   This has five sounds. It is like the English "sh" when at the beginning of a word or between vowels. Also, between vowels, it can sound like s in "some." It has the sound of z when in the prefix **ex** plus a vowel, but sounds like "eysh" when **ex** is followed by a consonant. In words of foreign derivation, it should be pronounced "ks," as in English. For example:
xadrez [shuh-'draysh] chess
queixa ['kay-shuh] complaint
trouxe [trose] I brought
exército [ee-'zehr-see-too] army
explicar [ey'sh-plee-'kahr] to explain
táxi ['tah-ksee] taxi

z   Pronounce this as in "zebra," except when it comes at the end of a word. A final **z** sounds like "sh." For example:
zanga ['zahn-guh] anger
fazer [fuh-'zayr] to do, to make
luz [loosh] light

Week 1

INTRODUCTION: SOME USEFUL PHRASES

Bom dia. [bon 'dee-uh]
Good morning.

Boa tarde. ['boh-uh 'tahr-de]
Good afternoon.

Boa noite. ['boh-uh 'noyte]
Good evening./Good night.

Eu chamo-me ...
['ay'oo 'shah-moome]
My name is ... (I am called ...)

Como se chama o senhor?
['kom-oo se 'shah-muh oo sen-'yor]
What's your name? (addressing a man formally)

Como se chama a senhora?
['kom-oo se 'shah-muh oo sen-'yor-uh]
What's your name? (addressing a woman formally)

Como se chama você?
['kom-oo se 'shah-muh 'voh-seh]
What's your name? (intermediate level of politeness, either sex)

Como te chamas?
['kom-oo te 'shah-mush]
What's your name? (informal, familiar)

Sou a sua professora. [so ah 'soo-uh proofe-'so-ruh]
I am your teacher.

Sou portuguesa. [so poor-too-'gay-zuh]
I am Portuguese.

O senhor é inglês? [oo sen-'yor eh eeng-'laysh]
Are you English? (addressing a man formally)

A senhora é inglesa? [uh sen-'yor-uh eh eeng-lay-zuh]
Are you English? (addressing a woman formally)

Eu moro em Londres. ['ay'oo 'moh-roo en ...]
I live in London.

Onde mora? [on'de 'moh-ruh]
Where do you live?

Fala português? ['fah-luh poor-too-'gaysh]
Do you speak Portuguese?

Não faz mal. [nah-oon fahsh mahl]
It doesn't matter.

Vamos agora aprender a falar português.
['vah-moosh uh-'goh-ruh ah-pren-'dair ah fuh-'lahr
poor-too-'gaysh]
We are now going to learn (to speak) Portuguese.

1.1 GENDER AND PLURAL OF NOUNS

1

All Portuguese nouns are either masculine or feminine. When you learn a new noun, try to remember its gender. Here are some rules of thumb to help you: nouns and adjectives ending in **-o**, **-im**, **-om**, and **-um** are generally masculine, while those ending in **-a**, **-ã**, **-gem**, **-dade**, **-ice**, **-ez**, **-ção**, **-são**, and **-ude** are feminine. Nouns ending in **-r**, **-l**, and **-e** can be either feminine or masculine. For more on gender, see section 5.1.

For example:
a flor (f.) the flower
but
o amor (m.) love
a capital (f.) the capital (city)
but
o capital (m.) capital (i.e., money)
a noite (f.) the night
but
o perfume (m.) perfume

The plural of nouns and adjectives is formed, in general, by adding **-s** to words ending in a vowel **(a/e/i/o/u)** and -**es** to words ending in a consonant. Words ending in **-m** change the **-m** to **-ns**. For other rules regarding how to form the plural, see section 5.2.

1.2 THE DEFINITE ARTICLE ("THE")

The definite article "the" is either **o** or **a**, depending on whether the noun is masculine or feminine, as you may have noticed in the examples above. The definite article also changes if the noun is plural, to **os** or **as**:

Masc. singular	**o**	**o perfume**
Masc. plural	**os**	**os perfumes**
Fem. singular	**a**	**a noite**
Fem. plural	**as**	**as noites**

Exercise 1

This exercise doubles as a vocabulary list. Use the rules in sections 1.1 and 1.2 to help you fill in the blanks with the appropriate definite article.

1	... rapariga	the young woman (in Brazil: moça)
2	... rapaz	the young man
3	... escritório	the office
4	... casa	the house, home
5	... flores	the flowers
6	... empregos	the jobs (employment)
7	... gatos	the cats
8	... alunas	the students (f.)
9	... mesa	the table
10	... mesas	the tables

IMITATED PRONUNCIATION

oo; oo per-'foo-muh; oosh; oosh per-'foo-mush; uh; uh 'noy-te; ush; ush 'noy-tush; ruh-puh-'ree-guh; ruh-'pahsh; sh-kree-'toh-ree'o; 'kah-zuh; flo'resh; en-'pray-goosh; 'gah-toosh; uh-'loo-nush; 'may-zuh; 'may-zush

In Portuguese, "a" and "an" are translated as **um** before a masculine singular noun and **uma** before a feminine singular noun. These articles also have plural forms: **uns** (m. pl.) and **umas** (f. pl.). These can translate as "some" in certain contexts.

Masc. singular	**um**	**um homem** (a man)
Masc. plural	**uns**	**uns homens** (some men)
Fem. singular	**uma**	**uma mulher** (a woman)
Fem. plural	**umas**	**umas mulheres** (some women)

Exercise 2

Use the rules you've learned so far to fill in the blanks with the appropriate indefinite article.

1	... viagem	a trip
2	... escritório	an office
3	... avião	a plane
4	... cidade	a city, town
5	... bilhete (m.)	a ticket
6	... homens	men
7	... mulheres	women
8	... viagens	trips, journeys
9	... escritórios	offices
10	... raparigas	young women

IMITATED PRONUNCIATION

oon; 'oo-muh, oon 'oh-men; 'oo-muh mool-'yair; oonsh; 'oo-mush; oonsh 'oh-mensh; 'oo-mush mool-'yairsh; vee-'ah-zhen; shkree-'toh-ree'o; uh-vee''ah-oon; see-'dah-de; beel-'yay-te; 'oh-mensh; mool-'yairesh; vee-'ah-zhensh; shkree-'toh-ree'oosh; ruh-puh-'ree-gush

VOCABULARY 1

Some greetings, farewells, and polite phrases:

Olá!	Hello!
Como está?	How are you? (polite)
Estou bem, obrigada.	(Woman's reply) I'm well, thank you.
Estou bem, obrigado.	(Man's reply) I'm well, thank you.
de nada	you're welcome, not at all
não tem de quê	don't mention it
Adeus! (in Brazil: **Até logo!**)	Goodbye!
Até logo!	See you later!
Até amanhã!	See you tomorrow!
faz favor	please, after you, please do, excuse me (drawing someone's attention)
por favor	please
faça o favor de ...	please ... (more formal)
se faz favor ...	if you please ...
Desculpe!	Sorry!
Com licença!	Excuse me! (e.g., if you need to get past someone)

1.4 USEFUL VERBS: **TER** ("TO HAVE")

The present tense in Portuguese can convey the English present tense (e.g., "I do") or the present continuous ("I am doing"). It can also be used to refer to the near future ("I'll do"): the context usually makes the time frame clear.

Here is the present tense of the verb **ter** ("to have"):

singular

eu tenho	I have
tu tens	you have (familiar)
você tem	you have (more polite)
o senhor tem	you have (most formal) (m.)
a senhora tem	you have (most formal) (f.)

ele tem	he has
ela tem	she has

plural

nós temos	we have
vocês têm	you have (familiar & polite)
os senhores têm	you have (most formal) (m.)
as senhoras têm	you have (most formal) (f.)
eles têm	they have (m.)
elas têm	they have (f.)

NOTE: As you can see from these conjugations, the Portuguese language has several possible registers when addressing someone, from familiar to very formal. More on this in section 1.8.

IMITATED PRONUNCIATION

'ay'oo 'ten-yoo; too ten'sh; 'voh-seh ten;
oo sen-'yor ten; uh sen-'yor-uh ten; ell ten; 'eh-luh ten;
nosh 'tay-moosh; 'voh-sehsh 'tay'en;
oosh sen-'yorsh 'tay'en; ush sen-'yor-ush 'tay'en;
'ehl-esh 'tay'en; 'ehl-ush 'tay'en

1.5 EXPRESSIONS WITH THE VERB **TER** THAT IN ENGLISH USE THE VERB "TO BE"

ter fome	to be hungry
ter sede	to be thirsty
ter frio	to be cold
ter calor	to be warm
ter sono	to be sleepy
ter razão	to be right
ter pressa	to be in a hurry
ter vinte anos	to be twenty years old

ter saudades to feel longing or nostalgia for, to miss:

Tenho saudades de Portugal.
I miss Portugal.

Another common expression is:

Que é que tem?
What's the matter with you?

ter de expresses a strong necessity or obligation
('to have to'):

Tenho de terminar este trabalho.
I have to finish this work.
Você tem de partir imediatamente.
You must leave immediately.

IMITATED PRONUNCIATION

tair fom*e*; said*e*; 'free'oo; kuh-'lohr; 'soh-noo;
ruh-'zah'o*n*; 'preh-suh, 'vee*n*-tee ah-noosh;
sau'oo-'dah-d'sh; poor-too-'gahl; kee''eh ke te*n*g;
'tun-yoo k*e* ter-mee-'nahr esht*e* truh-'bahl-yoo;
'voh-seh te*n* d*e* per-'teer eeme-'dyah-tuh-me*n*t*e*

1.6 SAYING "YES" AND "NO" AND FORMING QUESTIONS

1 The affirmative "yes" is **sim**:

Sim, tenho dinheiro.
Yes, I have money.

2 The negative **não** means both "no" and "not":

Não, não tenho dinheiro.
No, I don't have any money.

3 To ask a question, you usually simply give an enquiring
intonation to what would otherwise be a statement:

Fala inglês?
Do you speak English?

Tem troco?
Do you have (any) change?
Você quer mais vinho?
(Do) you want more wine?

However, when the sentence begins with a question word (e.g., "What...?"), the word order is reversed:

Que disse você?
What did you say? ("What said you?")

NOTE: The auxiliary verb "do" appears in the English construction of many of these sentences but does not exist in Portuguese. The verb "to do" (as in "To do" an activity) is **fazer**:

Que faz?
What are you doing?
Ela não faz nada.
She doesn't do/isn't doing anything.

(The verb **fazer** can also mean "to make.")

1.7 THE IMPERSONAL VERB **HAVER**

This is a useful verb that is mainly used for forms of "there is" and "there are." The third-person singular present tense **há** is used for both cases: the singular "there is" and the plural "there are." **Há** can also mean "ago" and "for" (relating to time).

For example:
Há muita gente aqui.
There are a lot of people here.
Há quanto tempo está em Lisboa?
How long have you been in Lisbon? ("There is how much time you are in Lisbon?")
O avião partiu há cinco minutos.
The plane left five minutes ago.

Haver de plus the infinitive of another verb expresses a strong intention to do something in the future. Its nearest equivalent in English is "I will":

Hei de ir ao Brasil. I will go to Brazil (some day).

present tense

eu hei de	I will ...	
tu hás de	you will ...	(familiar sing.)
você há de	you will ...	(polite sing.)
ele há de	he will ...	
ela há de	she will ...	
nós havemos de	we will ...	
vocês hão de	you will ...	(pl.)
eles hão de	they will ...	(m.)
elas hão de	they will ...	(f.)

IMITATED PRONUNCIATION

ah 'moon-tuh 'gen-te uh-'kee; ah 'kwan-too 'ten-poo sh-'tah en leesh-'bo'uh, oo uh-vee-'ah'oon per-'tyoo ah 'seen-koo mee-'noo-toosh; uh 'vair de; 'ay'oo ai de; too 'ahsh de; 'voh-seh ah de; el ah de; 'eh-luh ah de; nosh uh-'vay-moosh de; 'voh-sesh 'ah'oon de; ellsh 'ah'oon de; 'ehl-ush 'ah'oon de

1.8 SUBJECT PRONOUNS: "I," "YOU," "HE," "SHE," ETC.

Here are the Portuguese personal pronouns when they are used as the subject of the verb.

eu	I
tu	you (familiar sing.)
você	you (polite sing.)
ele	he, it (m.)
ela	she, it (f.)
nós	we
vocês	you (pl.)
eles	they (m.)
elas	they (f.)

Often the subject pronouns are omitted before the verb because the conjugation ending is enough to indicate who is doing the action (e.g., **Fala inglês?** "Do you speak English?"). When the subject pronoun is used, it is usually for emphasis or to avoid ambiguity.

The most informal register for addressing someone is **tu** ("you," familiar). This is used between friends, relatives, and people of the same age group who are on informal terms. It is seldom used in Brazil.

The more polite register **você** is used in situations such as employer to employee, teacher to student, etc., or if you don't know someone. It is widely used in Brazil.

The plural "you," **vocês**, is used when addressing more than one person where either **tu** or **você** applies (i.e., in both informal and more polite contexts).

The most formal way of saying "you" is **o senhor, a senhora, os senhores, as senhoras**. When talking to a mixed group of people, the masculine form is used.

Both **você** and **o/a senhor/a** take the third-person singular form of the verb (i.e., the same as **ele** and **ela**). **Vocês** and **os/as senhores/as** take the third-person plural (i.e., **eles/elas**). As mentioned above, the subject pronoun "you" may be omitted completely once the form of address has been established.

Falas português?
Do you (familiar) speak Portuguese?
Fala português?
Do you (polite & formal) speak Portuguese?

There is another plural "you" form, **vós**, but it is no longer used, except by elderly people in northern Portugal. You may also come across it in literature or prayers.

In referring to an individual who represents a group, a company, a shop, etc., use the plural "you" pronoun, **vocês**, with the appropriate verb form.

Again, note that the pronoun may be omitted:
(Vocês) têm os planos prontos?
Do you have the plans ready?
A que horas abrem?
What time do you open?

A big difference with English is that there is no neuter word for "it." You need to use **ele** to refer to a masculine object and **ela** for a feminine object. The same applies for the plural **eles** ("they," m.) and **elas** ("they," f.).

In English, "it" is also used in many impersonal expressions, such as "it is easy...." In similar expressions, Portuguese uses the verb on its own: **é fácil**.

Exercise 3

Translate the following, using the vocabulary you've already seen in the previous exercises and sections:

1 Tenho.
2 Você tem?
3 Não temos.
4 Vocês têm.
5 Ela tem?
6 Os senhores não têm.
7 Eles não têm?
8 I have no money.
9 Do you (f. sing. formal) have a ticket?
10 They (m.) have good jobs.
11 Do you (pl.) have a house?
12 You (sing. familiar) have an office.
13 We are hungry.
14 There is no table.
15 How long have you (sing. polite) been speaking English?

CONVERSATIONS

1 A **Bom dia. O senhor tem troco de cinco euros?**
   B **Agora não tenho, desculpe. Mas aquela loja à esquina tem troco, com certeza.**
   A **Muito obrigado.**
   B **De nada.**

2 A **Você tem tempo para um café?**
   B **Sim, tenho, com muito prazer.**
   A **Então vamos aqui ao lado. Têm um café muito bom e há pouca gente.**

3 A **Os seus amigos ainda têm o andar em Lisboa?**
   B **Agora não, mas têm uma linda casa no Algarve, com um grande jardim e piscina.**
   A **Que sorte! Quem me dera ter uma casa assim!**
   B **Eu também.**

TRANSLATIONS

1 A Hello. Do you have change for five euros?
   B I don't at the moment, I'm sorry. But that shop on the corner certainly has change.
   A Thank you very much.
   B You're welcome.

2 A Do you have time for coffee?
   B Yes, I do ("have"), with pleasure.
   A So let's go next door. They have great coffee and there aren't many people.

3 A Do your friends still have an ("the") apartment in Lisbon?
   B Not anymore, but they have a lovely house in the Algarve, with a big garden and a pool.
   A What luck! I wish I had a house like that!
   B Me too.

VOCABULARY 2

agora não	not at the moment
[uh-'goh-ruh 'nah-oon]	
desculpe [desh-'kool-pe]	I'm sorry (polite)
mas [mahsh]	but
aquele (m.) [uh-'kay-le]	that
loja (f.) ['loh-zhuh]	shop
esquina (f.) [esh-'kee-nuh]	corner
com certeza	definitely, certainly,
[kon ser-'tay-zuh]	for sure
tempo para ['ten-poo par-uh]	time for
muito prazer	with great pleasure
[moo'in-too pruh-'zayr]	
então [en-'tah'oon]	then, in that case
Vamos aqui ao lado.	Let's go next door.
[vuh-moosh uh-'kee	
ah'oo 'lah-doo]	
pouca gente	not many people,
[poh-kuh 'zhen-te]	few people
Os seus amigos ainda têm	Do your friends still
o andar em Lisboa?	have the apartment
[osh 'say'osh uh-'mee-gosh	in Lisbon? (polite)
uh-'een-duh 'tay'en oo an-	
'dahr en leesh-'boh-uh]	
lindo [leen-doh]	beautiful
grande [grahn-de]	big, large
jardim (m.) [zhuhr-'deen]	garden
piscina (f.) [peesh-'see-nuh]	swimming pool
Que sorte! [ke 'sohr-te]	What luck!, How
	fortunate!
quem me dera	how I wish ...
[ken me 'deh-ruh]	
assim [uh-'seen]	like that
eu também [ay'oo tahn-'ben]	me too, so would I

Note that adjectives are given in the masculine singular form.

Practice

Read and listen to the text using the vocabulary to help you, then answer the questions in the exercise. You can check your answers in the key at the back of the book.

PRACTICE TEXT

A senhora Smith é inglesa. Ela é de Londres, mas agora mora em Lisboa. Ela tem um bom emprego como auditora de uma grande empresa. Tem um escritório no Estoril. O marido dela é um bom professor de inglês. Eu sou portuguesa. Chamo-me Maria Helena. Sou do Algarve, mas agora moro em Lisboa porque sou médica em Lisboa. Lisboa é a capital de Portugal e é uma linda cidade.

VOCABULARY

ela é de	she is from
em	in
como	as
grande	large, big
no	in the
médico/médica	doctor (m./f.)
não	no, not
mas agora	but now (at present)
ela tem	she has
auditor/auditora	auditor (m./f.)
empresa (f.)	company
o marido dela	her husband
lindo	beautiful
porque	because

PRACTICE EXERCISE

Answer the following questions, basing your replies on the text you've just read.

1 A senhora Smith é portuguesa?
2 Onde mora agora?
3 Ela tem um bom emprego?
4 Como médica?
5 Onde tem ela um escritório?
6 Que faz o marido dela? (What does her husband do?)
7 A Maria Helena é de Lisboa?
8 Que faz ela?
9 Lisboa é a capital de Espanha?
10 Lisboa é uma cidade linda?

Week 2

- *two very important verbs: **ser** and **estar**, both meaning "to be"*
- *adjectives and how they must agree in number and gender with the noun they describe*
- *some important prepositions ("of," "in," "at," "for," etc.)*
- *addressing people using titles*
- *vocabulary for asking directions*

2

2.1 SER AND ESTAR: TWO VERBS FOR "TO BE"

Portuguese has two verbs that mean "to be": **ser** [sair] and **estar** [esh-'tahr] (for conjugation, see section 2.4). In general, **ser** denotes an inherent or permanent characteristic. It also refers to certain things that might be considered temporary, such as a profession or a stage in life: for example, **Sou uma aluna.** "I'm a student (f.)." **Sou um turista.** "I'm a tourist (m.)." **Sou solteiro/a.** "I'm single." In short, **ser** is used to describe what or who you are. The verb **estar** is used to describe temporary states or locations. Here are some examples:

Sou português/portuguesa. I am Portuguese (m./f.).
Lisboa é linda. Lisbon is beautiful.
Ele é casado. He is married.
Nós somos amigos. We are friends.

2.2 SER PLUS THE PREPOSITION DE

The construction **ser de** denotes possession or origin. However, if **ser** is followed by a possessive adjective or pronoun, **de** is omitted:

Eles são de Londres.
They are from London.
Esta chave é do senhor Gomes.
This key belongs to Mr. Gomes.
Esta casa é minha.
This house is mine.

2

Ser is also used to form the passive voice, in impersonal phrases, to give the time, and to describe a permanent location (e.g., of a well-known place).

For example:
Este trabalho é sempre feito por mim.
This work is always done by me.
É uma hora da tarde.
It is 1 p.m.
Onde é o castelo de Windsor?
Where is Windsor Castle?

2.3 THE USE OF ESTAR

The verb **estar** is used to describe a temporary state, action, or place.

Eles estão em Londres. They are in London.

Compare the above with **Eles são de Londres.** "They are from London." Notice that **ser** is followed by the preposition **de** and **estar** by **em**. This is a useful clue— with the preposition **em**, you know that **estar** must be used. Here are some examples of the usage of **estar**:

Ele está bonito. He is looking handsome. (temporarily)
But
Ele é bonito. He is handsome. (always)
Nós estamos cansados. We are tired.

Estar plus the preposition **a** followed by the infinitive is used to express the present continuous tense.

For example:
Eu estou a trabalhar. I am working.
(In Brazil, the present participle is used instead of the infinitive. Thus: **Eu estou trabalhando.**)

Estar com expresses the same meaning as **ter** in certain expressions.

Estou com fome. (= **Tenho fome.**) I am hungry.
Estou com sono. (= **Tenho sono.**) I am sleepy.

See also section 1.5.

2.4 PRESENT TENSE OF **SER** AND **ESTAR**

	ser	estar
eu (I)	sou	estou
tu (you, familiar)	és	estás
você (you, polite)	é	está
ele, ela (he, she, it)	é	está
nós (we)	somos	estamos
vocês (you, pl.)	são	estão
os senhores (you, formal m. pl.)	são	estão
as senhoras (you, formal f. pl.)	são	estão
eles, elas (they, m./f.)	são	estão

Here are more examples of the uses of **ser** and **estar**:

Ela é linda. She is beautiful.
Ela está linda. She is looking beautiful.
O homem é velho. The man is old.
O homem está velho. The man is looking old.
Elas são aborrecidas. They (f.) are boring.
Elas estão aborrecidas. They (f.) are bored.
Eu sou enganada por todos.
I (f.) am misled ("cheated") by everyone.
Eu estou enganada.
I am mistaken.

Remember that the present tense can be used to convey a variety of different time frames in Portuguese. It can correspond to the English:
• present tense (e.g., "I stay")
• present continuous (e.g., "I am staying")
• near future (e.g., "I'll stay")
The context should make the meaning clear.

2

In certain contexts, the present tense is used where English requires the present perfect: for example, in time expressions with **há** (refer to the explanation of the various uses of **há** in section 1.7):

Estou aqui há dois dias.
I have been here for two days. (lit. "I am here there are two days.")

IMITATED PRONUNCIATION

so; ehsh; eh; 'so-moosh; 'sah-oo*n* ...; ish-'to; ish-'tahsh; ish-'tah; ish-'tuh-moosh; ish-'tah-o*n* ...; 'lee*n*-duh; 'vehl-yoo; uh-boor-r*e*-'seed-ush; e*n*-guh-'nah-duh; poor 'to-doosh

Exercise 1

Practise using **ser**. Read through the list of vocabulary words that follows this exercise and then try to translate the sentences.

1 I (f.) am English.
2 Are you (formal) the manager of this hotel?
3 He is boring.
4 She is a secretary.
5 This is very important.
6 We (f.) are friends.
7 They (m.) are old.
8 Are these the suitcases? (meaning "your suitcases")
9 Estas malas não são minhas.
10 Isto é impossível.
11 Eu não sou secretária, sou professora.
12 Nós somos amigas.
13 Vocês são casados?
14 Eles são turistas?

VOCABULARY 1

inglês/inglesa [ee*n*-'glaysh/'glay-zuh]	English
gerente [zh*e*-'re*n*-t*e*]	manager (m.&f.)
deste ['daysh-t*e*]	of this
hotel (m.) [o-'tel]	hotel
secretário/a [s*e*-kr*e*-'tah-ree-oo/uh]	secretary
isto ['eesh-too]	this
importante [ee*n*-poor-'ta*n*-t*e*]	important
estes ['ehsh-tush]	these (m.)
mala (f.) ['mah-luh]	suitcase
minha ['meen-yuh]	mine (f. sing.)
impossível [ee*n*-poss-'ee-vel]	impossible
casado/a [kuh-'zah-doo/duh]	married
aborrecido [uh-boor-r*e*-see-doo]	bored, boring

Exercise 2

Now practice using **estar**. Translate:

1 I am in London.
2 Are you (f. familiar) tired?
3 She is not at home.
4 We are working every day.
5 They (m.) are mistaken.
6 The train is late.
7 I (f.) am bored.
8 Estou a comer./Estou comendo.
9 Você está em casa hoje?
10 Nós não estamos enganados.
11 O senhor está com fome.
12 Elas estão lindas.
13 As raparigas (Brazilian "moças") estão prontas.
14 Hoje, não estou no escritório.

VOCABULARY 2

Londres ['lon-dresh]	London
cansado [kan-'sah-doo]	tired
em casa [en-'kah-suh]	at home
trabalhar [truh-bul-'yahr]	to work
todos os dias ['to-doosh oosh 'dee-ush]	every day
comboio (m.) [kon-'boh'e-oo] (in Brazil, "train" is **trem**)	train
atrasado [uh-truh-'zah-doo]	late
comer [koo-'mayr]	to eat
hoje ['o-zhe]	today
fome (f.) ['fo-me]	hunger
pronto ['pron-too]	ready
escritório (m.) [esh-kree-'toh-re'oo]	office

2.5 ADJECTIVES: DESCRIBING THINGS

In Portuguese, adjectives need to agree in gender and number with the noun they describe. The adjective usually comes after the noun: **a língua portuguesa** ("the Portuguese language"). If the masculine form of the adjective ends in **-o**, this changes to **-a** in the feminine. If it ends in **-s**, **-z**, **-r**, you add **-a**. Adjectives ending in other consonants or **e** do not change. In the plural, adjectives are formed like plural nouns. (See also 5.1 and 5.2.)

When the adjective precedes the noun, its meaning may be different than when it follows the noun.

For example:
um homem pobre a poor man
(meaning he has no money)
um pobre homem a poor man
(an unfortunate man)

Before a noun, **grande** usually means "great." When it follows a noun, it means "big" or "large."

um grande homem a great man
(meaning distinguished)
um homem grande a big man
(referring to his physique)

There are some adjectives that are almost always placed before the noun: .

bom/boa	good
belo/bela	beautiful
mau/má	bad
longo/longa	long
breve	soon, short
muito/muita*	much
muitos/muitas	many

* When **muito** is used as an adverb, meaning "very much" or "very," it is invariable, with no feminine or plural forms.

The ordinal numbers ("first," "second," "third," etc.) also usually precede the noun, as in English: **no terceiro dia** on the third day.

Past participles (the -ed form of the verb) when used with **ser** or **estar** also need to agree in gender and number with the subject: **elas estão cansadas** they are tired.

2.6 PREPOSITIONS: "OF," "IN," "AT," "FOR," ETC.

de	of, from
em	in, on, at
a	at, to
por	for, by, through
para	for, to, in order to (see section 10.4)

Some of these prepositions combine with the articles:

de plus the definite article **o**, **a**, **os**, **as** becomes:
do, **da**, **dos**, **das** of the, from the

de plus the indefinite article is usually:
de um, de uma, de uns, de umas of a, of some
but you may also see **dum, duma, duns, dumas**

em plus the definite article becomes:
no, na, nos, nas in the, on the, at the

em plus the indefinite article becomes:
num, numa, nuns, numas in a, in some, etc.
(though the words are sometimes separated)

a plus the definite article becomes:
ao, à, aos, às to the, at the
(**a** does not combine with the indefinite article)

por plus the definite article becomes:
pelo, pela, pelos, pelas by the, etc.
(**por** does not combine with the indefinite article)

para does not combine with any article.

de, **em**, and **a** also combine with demonstrative
adjectives; for example, **nesta** in this (f.), **disto** of/from
this (neuter). And with third-person object pronouns, e.g.,
dele of/from him, **nelas** in them (f. pl.). As well as with
aqui, **ali**: e.g., **daqui** from here, **dali** from there, etc.
When **a** combines with **aquele, aquela, aquilo**, it
becomes **àquele** to/at that, etc. (see section 3.3).

SHOWING POSSESSION

Note that there is no equivalent of the apostrophe + s, as
in "Mary's house." Instead, use the preposition **de**:

a casa da Maria Maria's house ("the house of the Maria")

IMITATED PRONUNCIATION

d*e*, e*n*, uh, poohr, 'par-uh, doo, duh, doosh, dush, doo*n*,
'doo-muh, doo*n*sh, 'doo-mush, noo, nuh, noosh, nush,
noo*n*, 'noo-muh, noo*n*sh, 'noo-mush, 'ah'oo*n*, ah,
'ah'oo*n*sh, ahsh, 'pehl-oo, 'pehl-uh, 'pehl-oosh, 'pehl-ush

Exercise 3

Translate the following:

1 The book is on the table.
2 The woman is at the door.
3 She is going through the park.
4 Uncle Tomás's office.
5 I am on the (at the) telephone.
6 The water is in the glass.
7 I am here on vacation.
8 Vamos ao mercado.
9 Vou para casa.
10 Ela está na casa de banho.
11 Numa situação como esta.
12 Ele entrou pela janela.
13 Falo do acidente.
14 Ele deu o dinheiro ao rapaz.

VOCABULARY 3

livro (m.) ['lee-vroo]	book
mesa (f.) ['may-suh]	table
porta (f.) ['pohr-tuh]	door
ela vai ['eh-luh 'vah-ee]	she is going
parque (m.) [par-ke]	park
tio/tia ['tee-oo 'tee-uh]	uncle/aunt
telefone (m.) [te-'leh-foh-ne]	telephone
mercado (m.) [mer-'kah-doo]	market
água (f.) ['ah-goo'uh]	water
copo (m.) ['koh-poo]	glass
vou [voh]	I am going
casa (f.) ['kah-zuh]	home, house
casa de banho (f.) [buhn-yoo] (Br: **banheiro**)	bathroom
como esta ['koh-moo 'esh-tuh]	like this (one)
situação (f.) [see-too-uh-'sa'on]	situation
ele entrou ['eh-le en-'troh]	he came in
janela (f.) [zhuh-'neh-luh]	window

falo do ... ['fah-loo doo]   I'm talking about the ...
acidente (m.) [uh-see-'den-te]   accident
ele deu ['eh-le day'oo]   he gave

2.7 ADDRESSING PEOPLE USING TITLES

Sr. is the abbreviation of **Senhor** ("Mr.") and **Sr.ª** is the abbreviation of **Senhora** ("Mrs."/"Ms."). When politely addressing a married woman, you use her first name preceded by **Senhora (Sr.ª)** or **Dona (D.ª)**. If you don't know her first name, then **Senhora (Sr.ª)** followed by her family name is the usual form of address. Use the abbreviated form when writing. Unmarried women (up to a certain age) may be addressed as **Menina** plus their first name in Portugal. In Brazil, they are addressed by their first name, or **Senhorita** plus the first name or family name.

Just try to listen to how Portuguese people address each other in public and private contexts, and you'll gradually become familiar with the maze of Portuguese forms of address with their various degrees of formality!

When addressing a doctor (medicine, law, PhD), **Senhor Doutor (Sr. Dr.)** is used. For example: **Como está o Senhor Doutor?** How are you, doctor? (**Senhora Doutora** is used for a female doctor.) Generally, when addressing someone with a degree, use **Doutor/a**.

When addressing an engineer (university level), use **Senhor Engenheiro (Sr. Eng.º)** or **Senhora Engenheira (Sr.ª Eng.ª)**. An architect (university level) is **Senhor Arquiteto (Sr. Arq.º)** or **Senhora Arquiteta (Sr.ª Arq.ª)**.

VOCABULARY 4

Some useful phrases for asking the way and for giving directions:

Pode dizer-me, por favor, qual é o melhor caminho para ...?
Can you tell me, please, which is the best way to ...?

vá ...	continue ...
sempre a direito	straight on
sempre em frente	straight on
vire/volte à direita	turn to your right
vire/volte à esquerda	turn to your left
atravesse a rua	cross the road
chegando/ao chegar ao fundo	at (on reaching) the end
vê logo	you'll see
os semáforos	the traffic lights
a encruzilhada	the intersection
a bifurcação	the fork
a rotunda	the roundabout
a passagem de peões	the pedestrian crossing

Take careful note of the difference between **a direito** (straight on) and **à direita** (to your right, on the right). Getting this wrong could be problematic in finding the way to where you want to go!

You'll get a chance to use this vocabulary in the Practice section at the end of week 3.

Um encontro

2

SR. SMITH	**Olá, Dona Linda. Como está?**
SR.ª PEREIRA	**Estou bem, obrigada. E você?**
SR. SMITH	**Bem, obrigado.**
SR.ª PEREIRA	**Então por aqui?**
SR. SMITH	**Sim, estou aqui há dois dias, em negócios.**
SR.ª PEREIRA	**E quanto tempo vai ficar em Lisboa?**
SR. SMITH	**Vou ficar uma semana, pelo menos. Estou na casa dos meus amigos Bosomworth. Você lembra-se deles?**
SR.ª PEREIRA	**Sim, muito bem, por causa do nome. Creio que o nome deles quer dizer em português, 'peito de valor'. Que cómico!**
SR. SMITH	**Não é mais cómico que o seu, que quer dizer em inglês 'bonita pereira'.**
SR.ª PEREIRA	**Bem, é uma questão de opinião. Ah, aqui vem a minha amiga Angélica! Angélica, apresento-lhe o Sr. Tomás Smith ... Doutora Angélica dos Santos da Purificação.**
SR. SMITH	**Muito prazer, minha senhora.**
DR.ª SANTOS DA P.	**Igualmente.**
SR. SMITH	**Desculpe, por favor, repita o seu nome e devagar. Não compreendi bem.**
DR.ª SANTOS DA P.	**Angélica dos Santos da Purificação.**
SR.ª PEREIRA	**Bem, desculpe, Tomás, mas temos de nos ir embora. Estamos com muita pressa. Telefone-me. Adeus.**
SR. SMITH	**Adeus Dona Linda e pura Doutora Angélica. Até breve.**

A meeting between acquaintances

MR. SMITH Hello, ("Mrs.") Linda. How are you?

MRS. PEREIRA I'm very well, thank you. And you?

MR. SMITH Well, thank you. [Notice a man says **obrigado** and a woman says **obrigada**.]

MRS. PEREIRA Fancy meeting you here. (lit. "So by here?")

MR. SMITH Yes, I've been here for (lit. "I am here since") two days, on business.

MRS. PEREIRA And how long (lit. "how much time") are you going to stay in Lisbon?

MR. SMITH I'm going to stay for a week at least. I'm at my friends the Bosomworths' house. Do you remember them?

MRS. PEREIRA Yes, very well, because of their name. I believe their name (lit. "the name of them") means (lit. "wants to say") in Portuguese "bosom of worth." How funny!

MR. SMITH No funnier than yours, which means "beautiful pear tree" in English.

MRS. PEREIRA Well, it's a matter of opinion. Ah, here comes my friend Angelica. Angelica, let me introduce you to Mr. Thomas Smith … Dr. Angela dos Santos da Purificação.

MR. SMITH Pleased to meet you, ma'am.

SANTOS DA P. Likewise [lit. "Equally"].

MR. SMITH I'm sorry, please repeat your name, and slowly. I didn't understand [it] well.

SANTOS DA P. Angela of the Saints of the Purification.

MRS. PEREIRA Well, I'm sorry, Thomas, but we're going to have to go. We're in a hurry. Call me. Goodbye.

MR. SMITH Goodbye, Linda and pure Angelica. See you soon.

VOCABULARY 5

em negócios [en ne-'goh-see-oosh]	on business
pelo menos ['pay-loo 'may-noosh]	at least
lembra-se de ...? ['len-bruh-se de]	do you remember?
creio que ['kray-o ke]	I believe
quer dizer [kehr dee-'zayr]	it means
apresento-lhe [uh-pre-'zen-too-l'ye]	May I introduce to you ...
apresento-te [uh-pre-'zen-too-te]	(polite/fam.)
muito prazer	It's a real
['moo'in-too pruh-'zayr]	pleasure.
igualmente* (ee-gwahl-'men-te)	likewise

* This is a useful word for returning a compliment or reciprocating a wish, such as **Muito prazer.** (It's a pleasure.), **Boa sorte!** (Good luck!), **Feliz Natal!** (Merry Christmas!), etc.

Practice

Read and listen to the following text and then answer the questions in the exercise.

DIALOGUE

Na esplanada
It is 5 p.m. and people crowd the pavement cafés.
Complete strangers often share the same table. Paula
makes her way to a table where just one man is sitting.

PAULA   Está aqui alguém?

HOMEM   Não, não. Faz favor!

PAULA   Obrigada. Está tanta gente!

HOMEM   É verdade! E está tanto calor!

PAULA   [calling the waiter] Faz favor! Um chá forte com leite, um pastel de nata e um copo de água.

HOMEM   Desculpe, você é inglesa?

PAULA   Não, sou americana, mas vivo há muito tempo na Inglaterra. [She reaches across for the sugar.] Com licença! O senhor é português?

HOMEM   Não, sou brasileiro, mas minha família é portuguesa. Estou aqui em negócios. E você?

PAULA   Estou de férias e quero praticar o meu português.

HOMEM   Fala muito bem.

PAULA   Obrigada. Pode dizer-me onde são os lavabos?

HOMEM   Sim, são ali à sua direita.

PAULA   Muito obrigada e adeus. Vou pagar a conta ao balcão.

HOMEM   Adeus e boas férias!

VOCABULARY

aqui	here
alguém	anyone, someone
tanto	so much
gente (f.)	people
verdade (f.)	truth, true
calor (m.)	heat, hot
chá (m.)	tea
forte	strong
com	with

leite (m.)	milk
pastel (m.) de nata	a kind of custard tart
copo (m.) de água	a glass of water
mas vivo	but I live
vivo há muito tempo	I have lived for a long time
a minha família	my family
em negócios	on business
de férias/em férias	on holiday
e	and
quero	I want
praticar	to practice (to put into practice)
pode dizer-me	can you tell me (polite)
lavabos (m.)	toilets, restrooms
à sua direita	on your right
vou	I go, I'm going
pagar ao balcão (m.)	to pay at the desk (lit. counter)
conta (f.)	bill

PRACTICE EXERCISE

Answer the questions in Portuguese and then try to
reenact the dialogue out loud. Because the answers are
found in the preceding text, they're not included in the
key at the back of the book.

1 Que pergunta Paula ao homem?
(What does Paula ask the man?)

2 Está pouca (= few) gente?

3 Está frio?

4 Que deseja a Paula?

5 Ela é portuguesa?

6 Ela vive há pouco tempo na Inglaterra?

7 O homem é americano?

8 O homem está de férias?

9 Porque (= why) está Paula em Portugal?

10 Onde são os lavabos?

11 Onde vai ela pagar a conta?

Week 3

- *the present tense of three regular* **-ar, -er** *and* **-ir** *verbs:* **falar, comer, abrir**
- *question words ("who?," "when?," "why?," etc.)*
- *relative pronouns ("who," "that," "which," "whose," etc.)*
- *demonstrative adjectives and pronouns ("this," "that," "these," "those")*

3.1 PRESENT TENSE (REGULAR VERBS)

There are three groups of verbs in Portuguese, each of which conjugates with a certain pattern. The infinitives (e.g., "to do") in these groups end in **-ar**, **-er**, or **-ir**. To conjugate a simple (single word) tense, the infinitive ending is removed, and the conjugation ending is added to the stem. Below, the conjugation endings for the present tense are shown underlined. Because the subject pronoun is often omitted in Portuguese, the verb form indicates who is performing the action.

Present tense

	falar	**comer**	**abrir**
	to speak	to eat	to open
eu (I)	fal<u>o</u>	com<u>o</u>	abr<u>o</u>
tu (you, familiar)	fal<u>as</u>	com<u>es</u>	abr<u>es</u>
você (you, polite)	fal<u>a</u>	com<u>e</u>	abr<u>e</u>
ele, ela (he, she, it)	fal<u>a</u>	com<u>e</u>	abr<u>e</u>
nós (we)	fal<u>amos</u>	com<u>emos</u>	abr<u>imos</u>
vocês (you, pl.)	fal<u>am</u>	com<u>em</u>	abr<u>em</u>
eles, elas (they, m./f.)	fal<u>am</u>	com<u>em</u>	abr<u>em</u>

IMITATED PRONUNCIATION

'fah-loo, 'fah-lush, 'fah-luh, fuh-'luh-moosh, 'fah-law*n*;
'ko-moo, 'koh-m*e*sh, 'koh-m*e*, koo-'meh-moosh, 'koh-me*n*;
'ah-broo, 'ah-br*e*sh, 'ah-br*e*, uh-'bree-moosh, 'ah-bre*n*

Exercise 1

Translate, referring to new vocabulary below:

1 Procuramos uma casa.
2 Eles não falam português muito bem, mas compreendem tudo.
3 Ela nunca aceita o meu convite.
4 Que toma o senhor?
5 Ele abre a janela.
6 Estudo todos os dias.
7 Vocês não comem muito.
8 Parto às nove horas.
9 Os senhores trabalham muito.
10 As senhoras compram os bilhetes?

VOCABULARY 1

procurar [proo-koo-'rahr]	to look for
muito bem [moo'in-too ben]	very well
compreender [kon-pre-en-'dayr]	to understand
perceber [per-se-'bayr]	to understand/ perceive
tudo ['too-doo]	everything
nunca ['noon-kuh]	never
aceitar [uh-say-'tahr]	to accept
meu ['may-oo]	my (m. sing.)
convite (m.) [kon-'vee-te]	invitation
que [ke]	what
tomar [too-'mahr]	to take, to have (food or drink)
estudar [ish-too-'dahr]	to study
todos os dias ['to-doosh oosh 'dee-ush]	every day
partir [par-'teer]	to leave, to depart
às nove horas [ahsh 'noh-ve 'oh-rush]	at nine o'clock
muito ['mween-too]	very much, a lot
comprar [kon-'prahr]	to buy

Exercise 2

Translate, using the polite **você** form for "you" where appropriate:

1 My brother is looking for a job in Mozambique.
2 He is learning Portuguese.
3 Do you need help?
4 I accept your invitation with pleasure.
5 They eat and drink too much.
6 The train is leaving on schedule.
7 He is selling his car.
8 Today I'm not buying anything.
9 My sister doesn't eat at one o'clock.
10 She is on a diet.

VOCABULARY 2

o meu irmão [oh 'may-oo eer-'mah'oo*n*]	my brother
Moçambique [moo-sa*n*-'bee-k*e*]	Mozambique
aprender [uh-pre*n*-'dayr]	to learn
precisar de [pr*e*-see-'zahr d*e*]	to need
ajuda (f.) [uh-'joo-duh]	help
seu ['say-oo]	your (formal) (for a singular masculine object)
beber [b*e*-'bayr]	to drink
comer [ko-'mayr]	to eat
demasiado [d*e*-muh-zee-'ah-doo]	too much
partir [par-'teer]	to leave
a horas [ah oh-rush] (In Brazil: **no horário certo**)	on time, on schedule
vender [ve*n*-'dayr]	to sell
carro (m.) ['kahr-roo]	car
nada ['nah-duh]	nothing
a minha irmã [ah 'meen-yuh 'eer-ma*n*]	my sister
à uma hora [ah 'oo-muh 'oh-ruh]	at one o'clock
de dieta [d*e* dee-'ay-tuh]	on a diet

3

como ...? (adverb) "how ...?"

Como está?
How are you? (polite sing.)
Como se chama?
What's your name? (lit. "How are you called?")(polite sing.)
Como se diz "table" em português?
How do you say ("one says") "table" in Portuguese?
Como estão as peras?
How much are the pears?

como (conjunction) "as," "like"

Ela é como a mãe.
She is like her mother.
... como eu não queria dizer ...
... as I did not want to say ...

quando ...? (adverb) "when ...?"

Quando vais ao Brasil?
When are you going to Brazil? (fam. sing.)

quando (conjunction) "when"

Quando ele falou comigo ...
When he spoke with me ...

onde ...? (adverb) "where ...?"

Onde moram os senhores?
Where do you live? (formal pl.)
De onde vêm?
Where are you coming from? (pl.)
Por onde é a saida?
Where is the way out?

Note also the use of **aonde?** and **para onde?**
"where to?"

quem ...? (interrogative and relative pronoun) "who ...?," "whom ..."/"whose ..."

Quem foi que fez isto?
Who ("was it that") did/made this?
De quem é esta caneta?
Whose pen is this?
Não foi ele quem me disse ...
It was not he who told me ...

porque ...?, por que (adverb and conjunction)
"why ...?," "for what (reason)?"

Porque é que ele comprou esta casa?
Why did he buy this house? ("Why is it that he bought ...")
Por que motivo ...? For what reason ...?

Note also **porque não?** "why not?"; **porquê?** "why?";
porque (conjunction) "because"

que ...?, o que ...? (interrogative pronouns) "what ...?," "which ...?"

Que diz (você)? O que foi que ele fez?
What are you saying? What was it that he did?
Que rua? Which street?

que (relative pronoun) "that," "which," "whom"

O jantar que tive ... The dinner that I had ...
A mulher que você viu falar comigo ...
The woman whom you saw speaking to me ...

Note also **que** in exclamations, such as **Que chatice!**
"What a nuisance!" (slang), and also the interrogative
pronoun (used on its own) **Quê?** "What?"

quanto ...? (adverb, pronoun, adjective) "how much ...?"

Quanto custa?
How much does it cost?

Só Deus sabe quanto ela sofreu.
God alone knows how much she has suffered.

Note also: **quanto mais que ...** particularly/especially
as ..., because, and **quanto a ...** as to, as for,
regarding ...

quantos/quantas ...? (m./f.) "how many ...?"

Quantos quartos?
How many bedrooms?
Quantas libras deseja trocar?
How many pounds do you want to change? (polite sing.)

qual, quais (interrogative and relative pronoun, adjective,
conjunction) "which," "which one," "who," "whom,"
"what," "that" (denotes a preference, a limited number,
or emphasizes the subject)

Qual é o melhor hotel em Londres?
Which is the best hotel in London?
Quais são as calças que preferes?
Which are the trousers (that) you prefer? (fam. sing.)
**A irmã do meu amigo, a qual escreveu um livro
muito controverso.**
My friend's sister, (the one) who wrote a very
controversial book.

Note also: **cada qual** "each one," "each person," and **tal
qual ...** "just like ..."

Other relative pronouns are **cujo (m.)**, **cuja (f.)**, and
their respective plural forms **cujos** and **cujas** "whose,"
"of which," "of whom."

**A minha secretária, cuja mãe vive na América do
Norte, vai-se embora.**
My secretary, whose mother lives in North America, is
going away.
A sua carta, cujo conteúdo me surpreendeu ...
Your letter, the contents of which surprised me ...

IMITATED PRONUNCIATION

'ko-moo, 'kwan-doo, 'on-de, ken, poor-'ke, ke, oo ke
'kwan-too, 'kwan-toosh, 'kwan-tush, kwal, 'kwa'eesh,
'koo-zhoo, 'koo-zhuh, 'koo-zhoosh, 'koo-zhush

Exercise 3

Translate the following, using the polite **você** form for "you" where appropriate:

1 Qual é a estação mais próxima daqui?
2 Qual é a sua morada? (Also: "endereço," "direção")
3 Ela nunca faz o que eu quero.
4 Porque não vai de automóvel?
5 Creio que é muito longe.
6 Como vão os seus negócios?
7 Não sei a quem devo pagar.
8 Where are you going?
9 How much do I owe?
10 You haven't told me your name.
11 What did you say?
12 Who is that handsome man?
13 When are you going to France?
14 The keys (that) she gave me are not mine.

VOCABULARY 3

estação (f.) [ish-tuh-'sah'oon]	station
o mais próximo [oh 'mah-ish 'proh-see-mo]	nearest
daqui [duh-'kee]	to here, from here
morada (f.) [moo-'rah-duh]	address
nunca ['noon-kuh]	never
faz [fahsh]	he/she/it makes, does
quero ['keh-roo]	I want
vai ['vah-ee]	he/she/it goes
automóvel (m.) [ah'oo-too-'moh-vel]	car
creio ['kray-oo]	I believe
longe ['lon-zhe]	far
vão ['vah-oon]	they go
seus ['say-oosh]	your (formal) (for plural masculine objects)
negócios (m. pl.) [ne-'goh-see-oosh]	business
devo ['deh-voo]	I should/must, I owe (from **dever**, ought, should, must; also: to owe)
pagar [puh-'gahr]	to pay
não me disse [nah'oon me 'dee-se]	you didn't tell me (polite)
disse? ['dee-se]	did you say? (polite)
aquele (m.) [uh-'kay-le]	that (over there)
lindo ['leen-doo]	attractive
simpático [seen-'pah-tee-koo]	nice, charming
a França ['fran-suh]	to France
chave (f.) ['shah-ve]	key
ela deu-me ['eh-luh day'oo-me]	she gave me

DEMONSTRATIVES: "THIS," "THAT,"
"THESE," "THOSE"

this	these
este (m.)	**estes** (m.)
esta (f.)	**estas** (f.)
isto (indeterminate)	

that	those
esse (m.)	**esses** (m.)
essa (f.)	**essas** (f.)
isso (indeterminate)	

that (over there)	those (over there)
aquele (m.)	**aqueles** (m.)
aquela (f.)	**aquelas** (f.)
aquilo (indeterminate)	

When used after the prepositions **de** and **em**, the demonstrative adjectives and pronouns above combine to form one word as shown below. The demonstrative adjective **aquele/a** also combines with the preposition **a**.

For example:
de + **este** = **deste** of/from this (m.)
de + **aquilo** = **daquilo** of/from this (neuter)
em + **este** = **neste** in/on this (m.)
em + **essa** = **nessa** in/on that (f.)
em + **aquele** = **naquele** in/on that over there (m.)
a + **aquele** = **àquele** to/at that over there (m.)

Note that **a** only combines with **aquele/a**, etc.
(see section 2.6).

The neuter forms **isto**, **isso**, and **aquilo** are used to refer to objects with an unknown or indeterminate gender (for example, when referring to something abstract).

IMITATED PRONUNCIATION
'aysh-t*e*, 'aysh-t*e*sh, 'esh-tuh, 'esh-tush, 'ish-too,
'ay-s*e*, 'ay-s*e*sh, 'es-suh, 'es-sush, 'e-soo, uh-'kay-l*e*,
uh-'kay-lesh, uh-'keh-luh, uh-'keh-lush, uh-'kee-loo

Exercise 4

Translate the following:

1 Aquela loja à esquina.
2 Vamos àquela praia.
3 O que é isto?
4 Isto é um computador.
5 Por favor, feche essa porta.
6 Este é o meu marido e aquele é o meu filho.
7 Estas chaves não são minhas.
8 This house is large.
9 What is that? (unknown object)
10 I do not want those books over there.
11 This is impossible.
12 He is in that hotel.
13 This suitcase is that man's.
14 The tickets are in this handbag.

VOCABULARY 4

praia (f.) ['prah-yuh]	beach
computador (m.) [kon-poo-tuh-'dor]	computer
feche ['fay-she]	shut (imperative)
o meu marido [oh 'may-oo muh-'ree-doo]	my husband
a minha esposa [ah 'meen-yuh 'shpo-zah]	my wife
filho/a ['fee-l'yoo/yah]	son/daughter
mala (f.) ['mah-luh]	suitcase, handbag
carteira (f.) [kar-'tay-ruh]	handbag, wallet, school desk
grande ['gran-de]	large, big, great

CONVERSATION

Um telefonema

MARIA	Estou.
ANTÓNIO	Está lá? É a Maria?
MARIA	Sou sim. Quem fala?
ANTÓNIO	Daqui fala o António. Bom dia, como está?
MARIA	Bem, obrigada. E você e a sua família?
ANTÓNIO	Menos mal, obrigado. Estou muito cansado. Ontem à noite voltei de Londres.
MARIA	E então teve férias boas?
ANTÓNIO	Sim, mas o tempo estava péssimo.
MARIA	Você fez muitas compras?
ANTÓNIO	Não muitas. Está tudo tão caro! Mas comprei uma lembrança para você que, infelizmente, se quebrou na viagem.
MARIA	Não faz mal. Você é muito amável. Agradeço-lhe da mesma maneira.
ANTÓNIO	Aonde vai passar as férias este ano?
MARIA	Estou a pensar em ir a Londres também.
ANTÓNIO	Fala inglês?
MARIA	Não muito bem, mas faço-me compreender.
ANTÓNIO	Londres é uma grande cidade, e linda, mas está sempre a chover. Você terá de levar um guarda-chuva.
MARIA	Claro.
ANTÓNIO	Então, Maria, que há de novo? E sua irmã Emília? Que é feito dela?
MARIA	Mas eu não tenho nenhuma irmã.
ANTÓNIO	Você não se chama Maria dos Anjos da Silva?
MARIA	Não, chamo-me Maria da Conceição Lopes.
ANTÓNIO	Desculpe, enganei-me no número.

3

A telephone call

MARIA Hello? (lit. "I am")
ANTÓNIO Hello? (lit. "Are you there?") Is that you, Maria?
MARIA Yes, it's me. Who's speaking?
ANTÓNIO António (lit. "from here speaks António").
Good morning, how are you?
MARIA Well, thank you. And you and your family?
ANTÓNIO Not too bad, thank you. I'm very tired.
Last night (lit. "yesterday at night") I returned
from London.
MARIA And so did you have a good holiday?
ANTÓNIO Yes, but the weather was awful.
MARIA Did you do much shopping (lit. "purchases")?
ANTÓNIO Not much (lit. "not many"). Everything is so
expensive! But I bought a gift for you, which,
unfortunately, broke during the trip.
MARIA It doesn't matter. You're very kind. Thank you
all the same.
ANTÓNIO Where are you going to spend your vacation
this year?
MARIA I'm thinking of going to London too.
ANTÓNIO Do you speak English?
MARIA Not very well, but I make myself understood.
ANTÓNIO London's a great city, and beautiful, but it's
always raining. You'll have to take an umbrella.
MARIA Naturally.
ANTÓNIO Well, Maria—what's new? (lit. "What is of
new?") And what about your sister Emilia?
What's become of her?
MARIA But I don't have a sister.
ANTÓNIO Isn't this (lit. "don't you call yourself") Maria dos
Anjos da Silva?
MARIA No. This is (lit. "I am called") Maria da
Conceição Lopes.
ANTÓNIO Oh, I'm sorry. I have the wrong number
(lit. "I made a mistake in the number").

menos mal ['may-noosh mahl]   not too bad

ontem à noite   last night
   ['on-ten ah 'noy-te]

então [en-'tah-oon]   so, well, well then

férias boas (or **boas férias**)   good holidays
   ['feh-ree-ush 'boh-ush]

infelizmente   unfortunately
   [een-feh-leesh-'men-te]

Não faz mal.   It doesn't matter.
   ['nah-oon fahsh mahl]

É muito amável.   You are (or he/she
   [eh 'mween-too uh-'mah-vel]   is) very kind.

Agradeço.   (I) thank you.
   [uh-gruh-'da-soo]

da mesma maneira   all the same, in
   [duh 'maysh-muh   the same way
   muh-'nay-ruh]

este ano [aysh-t'uh-noo]   this year

claro ['klah-roo]   of course, certainly,
   obviously, it goes
   without saying

Que há de novo?   What's new? What's
   [kee ah de 'no-voo]   your news?

Que é feito dela?   What has become
   [kee eh fay-too 'deh-luh]   of her? What has
   she been doing?

Enganei-me. [en-guh-'nay-me]   I made a mistake.

Practice

Read and listen to the following text (if you need to, you can refer to the vocabulary list on page 41) and then answer the questions in the exercise.

3

DIALOGUE

A senhora Smith procura um banco e Centro de Turismo …

SR.ª SMITH   O senhor desculpe, dizia-me, por favor, se há um banco aqui perto?

TRANSEUNTE   Sim, há. Fica a dois minutos daqui. A senhora vai por aqui, sempre a direito e depois de passar uma garagem vê logo o banco.

SR.ª SMITH   Obrigada. Quero também ir ao Centro de Turismo. Onde fica?

TRANSEUNTE   Fica um pouco longe daqui. É melhor a senhora apanhar um táxi. A praça de táxis está ali à sua esquerda depois de virar aquela esquina.

SR.ª SMITH   E eles sabem onde fica o Centro de Turismo?

TRANSEUNTE   Claro, minha senhora, eles conhecem Lisboa como a palma da mão.

SR.ª SMITH   Muito obrigada.

TRANSEUNTE   De nada!

VOCABULARY

transeunte	passerby (m. & f.)
dizia-me	would you tell me
se há	if there is
um banco (m.)	a bank
perto	near
aqui perto	nearby
fica	it is (located) (see **ficar**, to stay, to remain, to be located, section 5.5)

sim, há	yes, there is/are
vai por aqui	(you) go this way
e depois de passar	and after passing
uma garagem (f.)	a garage
vê logo	you see right away
quero	I want
também	also, too
ir ao ...	to go to the ...
centro (m.)	center
onde fica	where it is (located)
um pouco longe	not far from here (lit. "a
daqui	little far ...")
melhor	better
apanhar	to catch (here, to take)
praça (f.) de táxis	taxi rank
ali	there
aquela esquina (f.)	that corner
e eles sabem ...?	and do they know ...?
	(verb **saber**)
claro	naturally, of course
conhecem	they know (see **saber,**
	conhecer section 6.2)
como a palma (f.)	like the back of one's hand
da mão (f.)	(lit. "palm of the hand")

PRACTICE EXERCISE

Complete the following sentences (the answers are in the key at the back of the book):

Desculpe, ... se ... um banco aqui ...? Fica a ... ...
.... A senhora vai ... ..., sempre ... ... e depois de ...
uma garagem ... ... o banco. Quero também ... ...
Centro de Turismo. Onde ...? Fica ... ... longe daqui.
É ... a senhora ... um táxi. A praça de táxis ...
... à sua ... depois de ... aquela .... E eles ... onde ... o
Centro de Turismo? ..., minha senhora, eles ... Lisboa
como ... ...

Week 4

- *possessive adjectives and pronouns ("my," "mine," "your," "yours," etc.)*
- *numbers (cardinal and ordinal)*
- *asking and giving the time*
- *days of the week*
- *months and seasons*
- *expressions for best wishes*

4.1 POSSESSIVES: "MY," "MINE," "YOUR," "YOURS," ETC.

In Portuguese, possessive adjectives and pronouns must agree in number and gender with the thing <u>possessed</u>: **o meu marido** my husband, but **a minha esposa** my wife.

	m. sing.	f. sing.	m. pl.	f. pl.
my, mine	**o meu**	**a minha**	**os meus**	**as minhas**
your(s) (fam.)	**o teu**	**a tua**	**os teus**	**as tuas**
your(s) (pol.)	**o seu**	**a sua**	**os seus**	**as suas**
his/her(s)/its	**o seu**	**a sua**	**os seus**	**as suas**
our, ours	**o nosso**	**a nossa**	**os nossos**	**as nossas**
your, yours	**o vosso**	**a vossa**	**os vossos**	**as vossas**
their, theirs	**o seu**	**a sua**	**os seus**	**as suas**

Since the forms **seu**, **sua**, **seus**, **suas** can mean "his," "her," "its," or "their" as well as "your" (formal), the forms **dele**, **dela**, **deles**, **delas** (literally "of him," "of her," "of them") are often used instead. For example:

o seu lápis his/her/your pencil
o lápis dele his pencil
o lápis dela her pencil

as suas casas his/her/your/their houses
as casas deles their houses
as casas dela her houses

Note that **dele**, **dela**, **deles**, **delas** reflect the number and gender of the <u>possessor</u> ("he," "she," etc.), and they

are placed after what is possessed (e.g., "houses").
In Portugal, a possessive adjective is normally
preceded by a definite article (e.g., **o meu copo** my
glass), although in Brazilian Portuguese, this is often
omitted. The possessive pronouns ("mine," "yours," etc.)
do not usually have an article (e.g., **isto é meu** this
is mine).

Unlike in English, in Portuguese when there is no doubt
about an object's ownership, the possessive adjective can
be replaced with the definite article. A common instance
is when referring to parts of the body or clothing.

For example:
Vou lavar as mãos. [voh luh-'vahr ush 'mah-oonsh]
I'm going to wash my hands.
Vista o casaco. ['vee-stuh oo kuh-'zah-koo]
Put on your coat.

Exercise 1

Translate the following:

1 Gosto muito da vossa casa.
2 Este é o seu copo e aquele é o dele.
3 A tua filha é muito simpática.
4 As nossas férias começam em junho.
5 A minha mulher chega sempre atrasada.
6 Vai lavar as mãos.
7 Vamos a casa deles.
8 Are these your (polite) suitcases?
9 My telephone is always out of order.
10 This is not mine.
11 I don't know their name.
12 Your (pl.) house is very far.
13 Our daughter is arriving tomorrow.
14 His friend (m.) is American.

VOCABULARY 1

gosto de ['gohsh-too d*e*]	I like
copo (m.) ['koh-poo]	glass
filho/a ['feel-yoo/yuh]	son/daughter
simpático [see*n*-'pah-tee-koh]	nice, charming
férias (f. pl.) ['feh-ree-ush]	holidays
começam [koo-'meh-saw*n*]	they begin
junho ['zhoon-yoo]	June
mulher [mool-'yeh*r*]	woman, wife
chega ['shay-guh]	he/she/it arrives
atrasado [uh-truh-'zah-duh]	late
avariado [uh-vuh-ree-'ah-doo]	out of order
não sei ['nah-oo*n* say]	I don't know
nome (m.) ['noh-m*e*]	name
longe ['lo*n*-zh*e*]	far
amanhã [uh-'muh*n*-yah*n*]	tomorrow
amigo/a [uh-'mee-goo/guh]	friend
americano/a	American
[uh-m*e*-ree-'kuh-noo/nuh]	

4.2 CARDINAL NUMBERS

1	um (m.), uma (f.)	19	dezanove
2	dois (m.), duas (f.)	20	vinte
3	três	21	vinte e um/uma
4	quatro	22	vinte e
5	cinco		dois/duas
6	seis	23	vinte e três
7	sete	30	trinta
8	oito	40	quarenta
9	nove	50	cinquenta
10	dez	60	sessenta
11	onze	70	setenta
12	doze	80	oitenta
13	treze	90	noventa
14	catorze	100	cem
15	quinze	101	cento e um/uma
16	dezasseis	102	cento e
17	dezassete		dois/duas
18	dezoito		

120	cento e vinte
125	cento e vinte e cinco
200	duzentos (m.), duzentas (f.)
201	duzentos/as e um/uma
300	trezentos/as
400	quatrocentos/as
500	quinhentos/as
600	seiscentos/as
700	setecentos/as
800	oitocentos/as
900	novecentos/as
1,000	mil
1,100	mil e cem
1,101	mil cento e um/uma
2,000	dois/duas mil
100,000	cem mil
1,000,000	um milhão
2,000,000	dois milhões

IMITATED PRONUNCIATION

(1–10) oo*n*, 'oo-muh, 'do'ish, 'doo-ush, traysh, 'kwah-tro, 'see*n*-koo, 'say'ish, sett, 'oh'it-too, 'noh-v*e*, daysh. (10–20) 'o*n*-z*e*, 'doh-z*e*, 'tray-z*e*, kuh-'tor-z*e*, 'keen-z*e*, d*e*-zuh-'say'ish, d*e*-zuh-'se-t*e*, d*e*-'zoh'it-too, d*e*-zuh-'noh-v*e*, 'vee*n*-t*e*. (30–50) 'tree*n*-tuh, kwar-'ren-tuh, see*n*-'kwen-tuh. (100, 200, 1000, 1,000,000) se*n*, doo-'zen-toosh, meel, meel'yah-oo*n*

Note that when 100 is used as a noun, it is **a centena**.
When 1,000 is used as a noun, it is **um milhar**. Here are a few examples of numbers used in sentences:

Já te disse centenas de vezes.
I have told you hundreds of times.
Estamos em dois mil e vinte e dois.
We are in 2022.
Quero dois selos; um de oitenta e oito cêntimos e outro de cinquenta e três cêntimos.
I'd like two stamps; one 88 cent stamp and the other a 53 cent stamp.
O meu pai faz hoje sessenta anos.
My father is sixty years old today.
(Note the use of the verb **fazer** in the Portuguese.)
Os nossos amigos chegam no dia vinte e oito de maio.
Our friends arrive on May 28.
(Note that the date is expressed by a cardinal number, "28," rather than an ordinal, "28th.")
Há dois meses que não como carne.
I have not eaten meat for two months.
(Note the use of **há** meaning "for," "since"—see section 1.7.)

4.3 ORDINAL NUMBERS

1st	**primeiro/a**
2nd	**segundo/a**
3rd	**terceiro/a**
4th	**quarto/a**
5th	**quinto/a**
6th	**sexto/a**
7th	**sétimo/a**
8th	**oitavo/a**
9th	**nono/a**
10th	**décimo/a**
11th	**décimo primeiro/a**
12th	**décimo segundo/a**
20th	**vigésimo/a**

30th	trigésimo/a
40th	quadragésimo/a
50th	quinquagésimo/a
60th	sexagésimo/a
70th	septuagésimo/a
80th	octogésimo/a
90th	nonagésimo/a
100th	centésimo/a
1,000th	milésimo/a
1,000,000th	milionésimo/a

4.4 ASKING THE TIME

Que horas são? What time is it?
(Note the use of **hora** (f.) "hour" when referring to the time of day, used in the plural, except to refer to one o'clock.)

São onze horas em ponto.
It's 11 o'clock on the dot. ("They are 11 hours ...")
São cinco horas e dez minutos.
It's ten past five.
São oito e meia.
It's half past eight.
São duas e vinte e cinco.
It's twenty-five past two.
São quatro e um quarto.
It's a quarter past four.
São vinte para as seis.
It's twenty to six. *OR*
Faltam vinte para as seis.
Colloquial, literally "twenty missing out of six" *OR*
São seis menos vinte.
Literally "six less twenty"
São cinco e quarenta.
It's five forty.
É uma hora.
It's one o'clock.
É meio-dia./É meia-noite.
It's midday./It's midnight.

Exercise 2

Translate the following:

1 Acabo o trabalho às seis horas.
2 Vamos passar quinze dias na praia.
3 Ela tem quatro irmãos.
4 O livro custa quinze euros.
5 Este elevador leva só cinco pessoas.
6 Vou a Paris de quatro em quatro semanas.
7 Faço anos no dia 20 de setembro.
8 He begins work at 8 o'clock.
9 She has two boys and three girls.
10 I write to my mother every five days.
11 He leaves on May 20.
12 He has not worked for ten days.
13 I am thirty-five years old.
14 It is a quarter to six.

VOCABULARY 2

acabo [uh-'kah-boo]	I finish
passar [puh-'sahr]	to spend
custa ['koosh-tuh]	it costs
elevador (m.) [ill-vuh-'dor]	elevator
leva ['leh-vuh]	he/she/it takes, carries
só [soh]	only
pessoas (f. pl.) [puh-'soh-ush]	people
de quatro em quatro semanas [... se-'muh-nush]	every four weeks
faço anos ['fah-soo 'uh-noosh]	my birthday is
começa [koo-'meh-suh]	he/she/it begins
escrevo [ish-'kre-voo]	I write
pai/mãe [pa'ee/mah'e*n*]	father/mother
trabalha [truh-'bahl-yuh]	he/she works
menino/a [m*e*-'nee-noh/nuh]	boy/girl (before puberty); **rapaz/ rapariga** after puberty)

domingo [doo-'meen-goo] Sunday
segunda-feira [se-'goon-duh 'fay-ruh] Monday
terça-feira ['tayr-suh ...] Tuesday
quarta-feira ['kwahr-tuh ...] Wednesday
quinta-feira ['keen-tuh ...] Thursday
sexta-feira ['saysh-tuh ...] Friday
sábado ['sah-buh-doo] Saturday

Hoje é domingo.
Today is Sunday.
Amanhã será segunda-feira.
Tomorrow will be Monday.
Depois de amanhã será terça-feira.
The day after tomorrow will be Tuesday.
Ontem foi sábado.
Yesterday was Saturday.
Anteontem (also: **antes de ontem**) **foi sexta-feira.**
The day before yesterday was Friday.

hoje à noite tonight
esta tarde this afternoon
esta manhã this morning
amanhã de manhã tomorrow morning
amanhã à noite tomorrow evening/night

daqui a quinze dias in two weeks
na próxima semana next week
(also: **na semana que vem**)
no mês passado last month
véspera the day before

4

4.6 MONTHS OF THE YEAR (**MESES DO ANO**)

janeiro [zhuh-'nayr-roo] January
fevereiro [fev-'rayr-roo] February
março ['mahr-soo] March
abril [uh-'breel] April
maio ['mah-yoo] May
junho ['zhoon-yoo] June
julho ['zhool-yoo] July
agosto [uh-'goh-stoo] August
setembro [se-'ten-broo] September
outubro [oh-'too-broo] October
novembro [noo-'ven-broo] November
dezembro [de-'zen-broo] December

4.7 SEASONS OF THE YEAR & GOOD WISHES

as estações do ano [ish-tah-'saw'insh ...]
   seasons of the year
a primavera [uh pree-muh-'veh-ruh] spring
o verão [oo ve-'rah'oon], **o estio**
   [oo ush-'tee-oo] summer
o outono [oo oh-'toh-noo] autumn
o inverno [oo een-'vehr-noo] winter
a Consoada Christmas Eve
o Natal Christmas
a Véspera de Ano Novo New Year's Eve
Ano Novo New Year
a Quaresma Lent
a Páscoa Easter

Feliz Natal! Merry Christmas!
Um próspero Ano Novo! A prosperous New Year!
Páscoa feliz! Happy Easter!
Parabéns! Happy birthday! (also: Congratulations! for a
   wedding, birth, etc.)
Boa sorte! Good luck!
Felicidades! Best wishes! (also: Many happy returns! lit.
   "Much happiness!")
Feliz aniversário! Happy anniversary!

Exercise 3

Translate the following:

1 Na próxima semana vou a casa da minha tia.
2 No mês passado o meu irmão foi para o Brasil trabalhar.
3 Os meus filhos chegam daqui a quinze dias.
4 Hoje à noite vamos ao teatro.
5 A primavera é a minha estação favorita.
6 Ontem esteve muito frio.
7 Depois de amanhã temos os resultados dos nossos exames.
8 I'm going to spend Christmas with my friends in Lisbon.
9 This year I have no vacations.
10 She is going to spend the summer in the Algarve.
11 Yesterday was hot.
12 My birthday is on Sunday.
13 Tomorrow morning I begin work.
14 July, August, and September are very hot months in Portugal.

4

VOCABULARY 3

foi [foy′*e*]	he/she/it went
vamos ['vuh-moosh]	we go
esteve [ish-'tay-v*e*]	he/she/it was
fez [faysh]	he/she/it made/ did
passar [puh-'sahr]	to spend time
férias (f. pl.) ['feh-re-ush]	holidays
faço ['fah-soo]	I do/make
começo [koo-'meh-soo]	I begin
meses muito quentes	very hot months
['may-zesh 'mwee*n*-too 'ke*n*-t*e*sh]	

Three conversations about the time and weather (all using the polite **você**, *as the first conversation is with a stranger, and the other two are acquaintances rather than people on close or casual terms).*

4

1 A Desculpe. Dizia-me, por favor, que horas são?
   B Desculpe, mas não lhe posso dizer as horas, porque o meu relógio está parado. Mas, oiça! Parece-me que o relógio da catedral está a dar horas.
   A Tem razão. Está, na verdade, a dar horas. São três horas.

2 A Estou muito preocupada.
   B Então porquê?
   A Já são seis e vinte e o meu marido ainda não chegou. Está sempre atrasado.
   B Não estou de acordo. No meu relógio tenho seis e um quarto. O seu relógio deve estar adiantado.
   A Não pode ser; o meu relógio está sempre certo. Além disso ouvi, ainda há pouco, as notícias das dezoito horas (18h00).
   B Nesse caso, é o meu que não está a trabalhar bem. Mas, quanto ao seu marido, não se esqueça que é a hora de ponta* e que é sexta-feira.
   A Já se faz tarde para o teatro. Há que tempos que eu ando a tentar arranjar bilhetes. Finalmente consegui. Mas, esta noite, o espetáculo começa às sete e quinze.
   B Ainda tem tempo. Olhe, aqui vem o seu marido.
   A Ainda bem!
   *In Brazil: **a hora do rush**

3   A   **Você acha que faz calor de mais no Algarve em junho?**

       B   **Não. Creio que ainda é suportável e as praias não têm tanta gente como nos outros meses do verão. Eu confesso que prefiro ir para o sul da Europa no outono. Não aguento o calor. E em outubro e novembro ainda há muito sol em Portugal mas não faz tanto calor.**

       A   **Eu só posso ter férias em junho; e, além disso, dou-me muito bem com o calor. Detesto a chuva, o vento e o frio.**

       B   **Eu também.**

4

TRANSLATIONS

1   A   Excuse me. Would you please tell me what time it is?

       B   I'm sorry, but I can't tell you the time because my watch has stopped. But listen—I think (lit. "it seems to me that") the cathedral clock is striking.

       A   You're right. It is indeed striking. It's three o'clock.

2   A   I'm very worried.

       B   Well, why?

       A   It's already twenty past six and my husband hasn't arrived yet. He's always late.

       B   I don't agree. My watch says it's (lit. "on my watch I have") a quarter past six. Your watch must be fast.

       A   It can't be. My watch is always right. Besides, I heard the six o'clock news a while ago.

       B   In that case, it's mine that's not working [well]. But, about your husband—don't forget it's the rush hour and that it's Friday.

       A   It's getting late for the theater. I've been trying to get tickets for ages. I finally managed to. But tonight the show starts at 7:15.

B You still have time. Look—here comes
   your husband.
A Thank goodness! (lit. "Just as well!")

3 A Do you think it's too hot in the Algarve in June?
   B No. I believe that it's still bearable, and the
      beaches don't have as many people as in the
      other summer months. I admit that I prefer
      to go to the south of Europe in the fall. I can't
      bear the heat. And in October and November it's
      still very sunny in Portugal (lit. "still there is
      much sun"), but it's not so hot (lit. "it does not
      do so much heat").
   A I can only have vacation time in June, and
      besides, I like ("I get on very well with") the
      heat. I hate the rain, wind, and cold.
   B Me too.

For Conversation 1

dizia-me* [dee-'zee'uh-me]	Could you tell me?, (lit. "Did you tell me?")
oiça ['oh'ee-suh]	listen ..., hear ... (imperative of **ouvir** to hear)
parece-me [puh-'reh-se-me]	it seems to me, it appears to me
dar horas [dahr 'oh-rush]	to strike the hour ("to give hours")
na verdade [nuh ver-'dah-de]	indeed, in fact, in truth

*This is the imperfect (a past tense) of the verb **dizer** [dee-'zayr] "to say," "to tell." In Portuguese, this tense is often used instead of the conditional.

4

For Conversation 2

estou muito preocupado/a [... pre'oh-koo-'pah-doh/duh]	I'm very worried
ainda não chegou [...'she-goh]	he/she/it has not yet arrived
estou de acordo [ish-'toh duh-'kohr-doo]	I agree
não pode ser	it can't be
além disso [ah-'len 'dee-soo]	besides that, besides
ainda há pouco [uh-'een-duh ah 'po-koo]	a while ago
nesse caso ['neh-se 'kah-zoo]	in that case
quanto a	as to, as for, regarding
não se esqueça ['nah'oon s'ish-'keh-suh]	don't forget ... (imperative)
hora de ponta/ hora de movimento [... 'pon-tuh/moo-vee-'men-too]	rush hour
já se faz tarde [zhah se fahsh 'tar-de]	it's getting late
há que tempos [ah ke 'ten-posh]	for ages

ando a tentar I've been trying
ainda tem tempo you still have time, there's still time

ainda bem thank goodness

For Conversation 3

não aguento [uh-'gwen-too]/ I can't bear, I can't
  não suporto [soo-'pohr-to] stand
dou-me muito bem com I get on very well
  ['do-me 'moo'in-too ben kon] with (from **dar-se bem**)

posso ['poss-soo] I can
eu também me too

Other Vocabulary

relógio (m.) [re-'loh-zhe'oo] watch, clock
atrasado [uh-truh-'zah-doo] slow, late
adiantado [uh-dee'an-'tah-doo] fast
certo ['sehr-too] right, correct
arranjar [uh-'ran-jahr] to get, obtain, arrange
bilhete (m.) [bee-'yeh-te] ticket
finalmente [fee-nahl-'men-te] finally, at last
conseguir to succeed, to
  [kon-seh-'geer] manage, to achieve
espetáculo (m.) show, performance
  [ish-peh-'tah-koo-loo]
achar ['ah-shur] to think
gente* (f.) ['zhen-te] people

*Note that **gente** ("people") is singular in Portuguese, so requires a singular verb, singular article, singular adjective, etc.: **a gente é** the people are. Colloquially, **gente** + the third-person singular of the verb has come to mean "we." Thus, **a gente é** = **nós somos**.

As you're getting more familiar with Portuguese, from now on, the translations of the conversations will no longer appear, apart from new expressions and words. We'll no longer provide the imitated pronunciation either, but you can always listen to the audio.

Practice

Read and listen to the following text and then answer the questions in the exercise.

DIALOGUE

No banco

SR. JONES   Bom dia!

FUNCIONÁRIA   Muito bom dia. Faça favor!

SR. JONES   Queria abrir uma conta, por favor.

FUNCIONÁRIA   Muito bem. Conta a prazo ou à ordem?

SR. JONES   Queria uma à ordem agora e mais tarde a prazo.

FUNCIONÁRIA   A taxa de juros agora está muito boa …

SR. JONES   Sim?

FUNCIONÁRIA   O senhor é residente em Portugal?

SR. JONES   Sim, decidi viver neste lindo país de que gosto muito.

FUNCIONÁRIA   Ainda bem! Faça o favor de preencher este impresso com o seu nome e morada nesta cidade e a sua última na Inglaterra; o nome do seu banco naquele país e o número da sua conta lá para obtermos referências. E, por último, a sua assinatura aqui em baixo.

SR. JONES   Aqui está o impresso com todos os pormenores e devidamente assinado. Preciso de dinheiro. Posso trocar as minhas libras aqui ou tenho de ir para aquela fila?

FUNCIONÁRIA   Não, pode trocar aqui.

SR. JONES   Como está o câmbio da libra esterlina?

FUNCIONÁRIA   A libra esterlina agora está mais baixa em relação ao Euro. Está a sessenta e quatro cêntimos. Aqui tem a sua ficha, número 41. Dirija-se ali à caixa nº. 3 e espere que chamem o seu número para receber o dinheiro.

VOCABULARY

funcionário/a	employee, civil servant
queria	I would like, I wanted (**queria** is the imperfect tense of **querer** "to want"; this tense is often used in place of the conditional)
muito bem	very well
conta (f.) a prazo	deposit account
conta (f.) à ordem	current account
(in Brazil: **a conta corrente**)	
mais tarde	later (on)
Sim?	Yes?, Really?
taxa (f.) de juros	the interest rate
muito bom/boa	very good (m./f.)
decidi	I decided
viver	to live
país (m.)	country, nation
de que gosto muito	that I like so much
Ainda bem!	So glad! (also "Fortunately!" or, by changing the intonation, "Just as well!")
preencher este impresso (m.)	to fill in this form
último	last
lá	there (over there)
para obtermos	so that we get
por último	lastly
assinatura (f.)	signature
aqui em baixo	down here (at the bottom)
pormenor (m.)	detail
devidamente assinado	duly signed
precisar (de)	to need
dinheiro (m.)	money
Posso trocar as minhas libras (f.)?	Can I exchange my pounds?
ou	or
ir	to go
fila (f.)	queue

Como está o câmbio?	What is the exchange rate?
ficha (f.)	numbered token, record
número (m.)	number
dirigir-se	to head for
caixa (f.)	cashier, cash desk
esperar	to wait
que chamem	that they call
receber	to receive

PRACTICE EXERCISE

Complete the following sentences, looking back at the text in the dialogue to choose which words to put in the spaces:

1 Queria … uma ….

2 Conta a … ou … …?

3 A taxa de … agora … … ….

4 Sim, decidi … neste … … de que … ….

5 Faça o favor de …este … com o seu nome e … nesta … e a sua … na Inglaterra; o … do seu banco … país e o … da sua conta … para … … E, por último, a sua … aqui … ….

6 Aqui está o … com … … … e devidamente … … de dinheiro. Posso … as minhas libras … ou … … … para … …?

7 A … está o câmbio da … …?

8 A libra hoje está … … Aqui … a sua …, número 41. Dirija-se ali à … 3 e espere que … o seu … para … o dinheiro.

Week 5

- feminine and plural forms of nouns and adjectives
- the preterite tense (simple past) in regular **-ar**, **-er**, and **-ir** verbs
- giving commands (the imperative) in both regular and irregular verbs
- useful verbs: **andar** and **ficar**

5.1 FORMING THE FEMININE

As we've seen, nouns in Portuguese are either masculine or feminine, and certain other parts of speech, such as articles and adjectives, have to agree with the gender. Nouns that refer to people or animals typically change form to indicate the gender, with a final **-a** usually indicating a female. For example:

o gato, a gata cat
o velho, a velha old man, old woman
António, Antónia
pintor, pintora painter
francês, francesa French
espanhol, espanhola Spanish
alemão, alemã German

However, there are some variants and exceptions to this pattern.

Firstly, there are certain nouns, chiefly of Greek origin, that end in **-a** but are masculine.

These include:
o tema theme
o sistema system
o clima climate
o telefonema telephone call
o quilograma kilogram
o panorama panorama, view
o poeta poet (a female poet is **a poetisa**)
o dia day
o mapa map

The noun **criança** ("child") is always preceded by the feminine article (**a criança**) and refers to both sexes.

Nouns and adjectives ending in **-e** generally do not change form, but the preceding article needs to be masculine or feminine to indicate the gender:

o estudante, a estudante student (m. & f.)
o lápis verde the green pencil
a caneta verde the green pen
um quarto grande a large bedroom
uma sala grande a large living room

As mentioned in week 4, **gente** ("people") is always singular. It is feminine and is always preceded by a feminine article: **a gente**.

Nouns and adjectives ending in **-ista** also refer to both genders; just the preceding article changes:

o pianista, a pianista pianist
o artista, a artista artist, performer
o jornalista, a jornalista journalist
o vigarista, a vigarista crook, swindler
o dentista, a dentista dentist

Adjectives ending in a consonant generally don't change form for gender (although they do have a plural form):
um homem agradável a pleasant man
uma mulher agradável a pleasant woman
o rapaz está feliz the young man is happy
a rapariga está feliz the young woman is happy
uma lição simples an easy lesson
um caso simples a simple case

-eu usually changes to **-eia**:
Europeu, Europeia European

Some nouns ending in **-or** change to **-riz**:
ator, atriz actor, actress
embaixador, embaixatriz ambassador (m. & f.)

Other **-or** words add an **-a** for the feminine:

embaixadora ambassador (f.)
encantador, encantadora charming man/woman

Adjectives that end in **-u** (not **-eu**) form their feminine by adding **-a**. For example:

cru, crua raw, uncooked (m. & f.)
nu, nua naked, bare (m. & f.)

Nouns ending in **-ão** generally lose the **-o** in the feminine. Some irregular nouns, however, change to **-ona**, while **cão** is an exception to any rule:

comilão, comilona glutton (m. & f.)
mandrião, mandriona lazy man/woman
cão, cadela dog, bitch

Some irregular adjectives include:

mau, má   bad (m. & f.)
bom, boa   good (m. & f.)
dois, duas   two (m. & f.)

In certain nouns, the feminine is altogether different from its masculine counterpart or changes in ways that don't follow the previously described patterns:

homem, mulher man, woman
pai, mãe father, mother
avô, avó grandfather, grandmother

Exercise 1

Fill in the blanks:

1 Hoje o tempo está .... (bad).

2 Ela é uma ... . (good athlete).

3 Não sei onde está ... ... (my French map).

4 ... ... (My sister) é mais ... (old) do que eu.

5 ... ... (My friend, f.) é ... (Spanish) mas o marido dela é .... (English).

6 É uma ... ... (good thing) que (você) faz.

7 Há ... ... (many pleasant people) neste mundo.

8 O meu colega está muito ... (happy) no Brasil.

9 É uma instituição .... (European).

10 A mãe da minha amiga é ... .(a poet).

11 Tenho um ... ... (large green car).

12 O meu primo é um ... ... (good writer) e a mulher dele é também .... (writer).

13 O António é um ... . (Portuguese journalist).

14 Esta galinha está .... (uncooked).

VOCABULARY 1

tempo (m.)	weather, time (general)
atleta	athlete (m. & f.)
não sei	I don't know (from **saber**, to know)
coisa (f.)	thing
simpático	pleasant, nice
contente	happy
neste mundo	in this world
escritor/ escritora	writer
primo/a	cousin
jornalista	journalist (m. & f.)
galinha (f.)	chicken, hen

5.2 FORMING THE PLURAL

To form the plural, we've seen that the general rule is to add an **-s** to words ending in a vowel and **-es** to words ending in **-r**, **-s**, and **-z**.

For example:
casa becomes **casas**
amante becomes **amantes** (lovers)
feliz becomes **felizes**
flor becomes **flores**
francês becomes **franceses**

Note that nouns and adjectives ending in **-ês** lose the circumflex accent in the plural.

In nouns and adjectives ending in **-m**, this changes to **-ns** in the plural.

For example:
o homem (man) becomes **os homens** (men)
a viagem (journey) becomes **as viagens** (journeys)

In nouns and adjectives ending in **-al**, **-el**, **-ol**, and **-ul**, the **-l** changes to **-is** in the plural.

For example:
a capital (capital) becomes **as capitais** (capitals)
espanhol becomes **espanhóis** (Spanish)
o papel (paper) becomes **os papéis** (papers)
azul becomes **azuis** (blue)

When the noun ends in **-el** or **-ol** in the singular, the plural ending takes an acute accent for phonetic reasons. In certain words, the vowel sound can also change in the plural. This can occur in masculine words with an **o** in the second-to-last syllable: this letter has a closed vowel sound in the singular but an open vowel sound in the feminine and plural.

For example:
formoso, formosa, formosos (beautiful)

There are also a few nouns and adjectives that end in **-s** in the singular—they don't change in the plural:

um lápis (pencil) > **dois lápis**
um caso simples (a simple case) > **uns casos simples**

Words ending in **-il** form the plural in two different ways, depending on whether the **-il** is stressed or not. If stressed, **-il** is changed to **-is**. For example:

civil > **civis**

If unstressed, **-il** is changed to **-eis**. For example:

fácil > **fáceis**

Nouns and adjectives ending in **-ão** form the plural in one of three ways:

-ão to **-oes**
This is the most usual plural form for -**ão** words. For example:

o limão (lemon) > **os limões**
a lição (lesson) > **as lições**
o leão (lion) > **os leões**

-ão to **-ães**
The most common nouns following this rule are:

o capitão (captain) > **os capitães**
o alemão (German) > **os alemães**
o cão (dog) > **os cães**
o pão (bread) > **os pães**

-ão to **-ãos**
There are very few words that take this plural form. The most common are the following:

o irmão (brother) > **os irmãos**
a mão (hand) > **as mãos**

o cristão (Christian) > **os cristãos**
o órfão (orphan) > **os órfãos**
o cidadão (citizen) > **os cidadãos**

Note that in Portuguese, the masculine plural is used for a mixed-gender situation. For example, **os pais** can mean "fathers" but frequently means "parents." Similarly, **filhos** can mean "sons" but can also refer to one's sons and daughters; **tios** can mean "uncle and aunt," etc.

Exercise 2

Translate the following:

1 Two living rooms.
2 My brother and sister.
3 The flowers are beautiful.
4 These problems are difficult.
5 In the summer, there are many people on the beaches.
6 Three English students.
7 Four sheets.
8 My friends (m. & f.) are very kind.
9 I don't know these men.
10 The German children do not like dogs.
11 I buy five loaves of bread every day.
12 She likes all animals.
13 My sister has blue eyes.
14 I have dirty hands.
15 These lemons are good.
16 My parents are always so happy.

VOCABULARY 2

sala (f.)/sala de estar	living room, lounge
lindo	pretty, beautiful
problema (m.)	problem
praia (f.)	beach
lençol (m.)	sheet
amável	kind, nice
não conheço	I don't know (am not familiar with)
criança (f.)	child (used for both genders)
todo	all
olho (m.)	eye
sujo	dirty
saúde (f.)	health
tão	so, as
gostar de	to like

5.3 THE PRETERITE

The preterite is the equivalent of the simple past (e.g., "I spoke," "I ate," "I opened"). Here are its regular conjugation endings for **-ar**, **-er** and **-ir** verbs:

	falar to speak	**comer** to eat	**abrir** to open
eu	fal**ei**	com**i**	abr**i**
tu	fal**aste**	com**este**	abr**iste**
ele, ela, você	fal**ou**	com**eu**	abr**iu**
nós	fal**ámos**	com**emos**	abr**imos**
eles, vocês	fal**aram**	com**eram**	abr**iram**

It is used to convey a completed action in the past. It can also translate to the English present perfect ("I have spoken," "I have eaten," "I have opened"), but only when the action is completely finished: **Eles partiram para a praia.** They have left for the beach.

Exercise 3

Translate:

1 Ontem recebi uma carta da minha amiga.
2 Nós gostámos muito da sua casa.
3 Na semana passada, visitámos uma escola muito moderna.
4 Eles partiram para o Brasil.
5 Vocês já venderam a vossa casa?
6 Não, ainda não vendemos a nossa casa.
7 Eles ainda não escreveram.
8 I did not understand.
9 What did they drink?
10 I have already eaten.
11 When did they leave?
12 At what time did the train leave?
13 We didn't open the window.
14 He didn't eat last night.
15 Did you (polite) speak to your mother?
16 I met (knew) your brother in Lisbon.

VOCABULARY 3

beber	to drink
já	already
a que horas	at what time
chegar	to arrive
janela (f.)	window
ontem à noite	last night
pai/mãe	father/mother
conhecer*	to know, to meet
Lisboa	Lisbon

*The verb **conhecer** ("to know" in the sense of "to be familiar with") is used in Portuguese to express "to meet someone for the first time"—on being introduced, for example. In other situations, the verb "to meet" is normally **encontrar**. See section 6.2 for more on **conhecer**.

To make a command or request, there are different forms, depending on who is being addressed: **tu** (familiar sing.), **você** (polite sing.), **nós** ("us"), or **vocês** (plural). Here are the regular imperative forms for **-ar**, **-er**, and **-ir** verbs:

	falar to speak	**comer** to eat	**abrir** to open
(tu)	**Fala!** Speak!	**Come!** Eat!	**Abre!** Open!
(você)	**Fale!**	**Coma!**	**Abra!**
(nós)	**Falemos!**	**Comamos!**	**Abramos!**
(vocês)	**Falem!**	**Comam!**	**Abram!**

The **nós** imperative translates to "Let's ..." (e.g., **Vamos!** Let's go!).

Note that all the forms except for the **tu** imperative are the same as the present subjunctive (see section 9.1).

The present subjunctive is also used for the imperative of the familiar **tu** in negative commands ("Don't ..."). For example:

Não fales tanto! Don't talk so much!
Não faças isso! Don't do that!

IRREGULAR VERBS

With certain exceptions, the imperative of irregular verbs is formed from the stem of the first-person singular of the present indicative (the present tense) plus the endings shown below for some common irregular verbs:

	ver to see	**trazer** to bring	**fazer** to do	**dar** to give
(você)	**Veja!**	**Traga!**	**Faça!**	**Dê!**
(vocês)	**Vejam!**	**Tragam!**	**Façam!**	**Deem!**
(nós)	**Vejamos**	**Tragamos**	**Façamos**	**Dêmos**

5

	dizer	**ser**	**estar**	**querer**
	to say	to be	to be	to want
(você)	Diga!	Seja!	Esteja!	Queira!
(vocês)	Digam!	Sejam!	Estejam!	Queiram!
(nós)	Digamos	Sejamos	Estejamos	Queiramos

	ter	**vir**	**ir**	**pôr**
	to have	to come	to go	to put
(você)	Tenha!	Venha!	Vá!	Ponha!
(vocês)	Tenham!	Venham!	Vão!	Ponham!
(nós)	Tenhamos	Venhamos	Vamos	Ponhamos

Here is the **tu** affirmative imperative for some common irregular verbs: **Vê!** "See!," **Faz!** "Do!"/"Make!," **Traz!** "Bring!," **Dá!** "Give!," **Diz!** "Speak!," **Está!** "Be!," **Tem!** "Have!," **Vem!** "Come!," **Vai!** "Go!," **Põe!** "Put!"

Exercise 4

Translate (use **você** for "you," sing.):

1 Venha cá.
2 Fale devagar.
3 Não faça barulho.
4 Vá por ali.
5 Não seja tonto.
6 Esteja quieto.
7 Traga a lista dos vinhos.
8 Speak slowly.
9 Let's open the window.
10 Shut (pl.) the door.
11 Don't eat (pl.) so quickly.
12 Let's see …
13 Come (pl.) at once.
14 Let's go!
15 Don't speak (pl.) so loudly.
16 Don't say anything.

VOCABULARY 4

cá	here
devagar	slowly
barulho (m.)	noise
por ali	that way, over there, through there
tonto	silly
quieto	quiet, still
lista (f.)	list
vinho (m.)	wine
fechar	to close
tão depressa	as quickly
já	already, at once, right away
nada	nothing
ali	there
alto	loud, high, tall

5.5 USEFUL VERBS: ANDAR AND FICAR

Apart from **ser** and **estar**, certain other verbs can translate "to be" in Portuguese. One example is **andar**, which literally means "to go" or "to walk," but when used with another verb acts as a verb of "movement": in respect not only to space but also to time. So, when it is used instead of **estar**, it conveys the idea of a continuing action over a certain period of time. For example:

ando a tentar I have been trying (over time)
ela anda grávida she is pregnant

The verb **andar** is also used (rather than **ir**) for many types of transportation and movement. For example:

andar a pé	to walk
andar a cavalo	to ride, to go on horseback
andar de avião	to fly
andar de barco	to go by boat
andar de comboio	to go by train
andar de carro	to drive, to go by car

The verb **ficar**, which literally means "to stay" or "to remain," can also mean "to be" in certain contexts. For example, it is used to describe locations:

Onde fica o Centro de Turismo?
Where is the Tourist Office?
(In this case, you could equally use either **estar** or **ser**.)

You'll also often find **ficar** used rather than **estar** in expressions of emotion resulting from some news:

Fiquei tão contente ao ler a tua carta.
I was so pleased to read your letter.

Note also the following uses:

Fico à espera da tua resposta.
I await ("remain waiting for") your reply.
Vou ficar naquela casa.
I am going to stay in that house.

ficar com to keep, to have:

Fico com as chaves.
I'll keep the keys.
Fico com este.
I'll have this one.

ficar bem/mal to suit/not to suit, to pass/not to pass an exam:

Esta cor fica-lhe bem.
This color suits you.
Ela ficou bem no exame.
She passed the exam.
Ela ficou mal no exame.
She failed the exam.

Um emprego em Moçambique / A job in Mozambique

LUÍSA A tua irmã Ana sempre conseguiu o tal emprego em Moçambique?

JOÃO Sim, recebeu a resposta há duas semanas, depois de muitas entrevistas e de esperar seis meses. Está nas suas sete quintas, porque já temia não ser aceite. O ordenado é bom, mas o que mais lhe agrada é a oportunidade de conhecer um país em vias de desenvolvimento.

LUÍSA Que género de trabalho é? Não me lembro do que ela me disse.

JOÃO Ela vai dar aulas de matemática numa escola secundária. Aparentemente, há lá falta de professores. Já está tudo organizado. Só falta o visto. Sabes que ela vai primeiro a Lisboa por dois meses para um curso de verão com todas as despesas pagas?

LUÍSA Não, não sabia nada disto. Que bom!

JOÃO É verdade. Tanto mais que o noivo também espera ir para lá. Precisam de engenheiros civis. Ele respondeu a um anúncio e agora está à espera de resposta. Tanto ele como a Ana querem conhecer a África.

LUÍSA Mas ele fala português?

JOÃO Fala sim, e fluentemente. Ele tirou um curso de português há anos, e depois esteve a trabalhar em Lisboa uns anos.

LUÍSA E quando se casam?

JOÃO Tencionam casar-se daqui a dois anos se tudo correr bem.

LUÍSA Quando parte a Ana para Lisboa?

JOÃO Na próxima quinta-feira, no voo da TAP Air Portugal. Oxalá não haja nevoeiro ou greves.

LUÍSA Vou telefonar-lhe esta noite a desejar-lhe boa sorte. Adeus, até à vista.

5

tal	such, that
receber	to receive
conseguir	to get, to obtain
conseguir + infinitive	to manage to …, to succeed in …
sempre	always, after all, in the end, finally
sempre conseguiu (idiomatic use of **sempre**)	in the end she obtained
responder	to reply
resposta (f.)	answer, reply
há duas semanas	two weeks ago
há anos	years ago (see **haver** in section 1.7)
depois de	after
entrevista (f.)	interview
quinta (f.)	farm
Está nas suas sete quintas.	He/she is in seventh heaven/over the moon. (lit. "in his/her seven farms")
aula (f.)	lesson, course
temer	to dread
aceitar	to accept
ser aceite	to be accepted
ordenado (m.)	salary
agradar	to please
o que mais lhe agrada …	what pleases her most …
país (m.) em vias de desenvolvimento	developing country
género (m.)	type, kind
lembrar-se de	to remember
ensinar	to teach
escola (f.) secundária	secondary school
faltar	to be lacking, to be missing
falta (f.)	shortage
Há lá falta.	There is a shortage over there.

organizar	to organize
Já está tudo organizado.	Everything is already organized.
visto (m.)	visa
curso (m.) de verão	summer course
despesas (f.)	expenses
todas as despesas pagas	all expenses paid
saber	to know (a fact)
Não sabia nada disto.	I didn't know anything about it.
Que bom!	How great!
verdade (f.)	truth
É verdade.	That's right. That's true.
tanto mais	besides, moreover, particularly as
noivo/a	fiancé, bridegroom/ fiancée, bride
esperança (f.)	hope
precisar de	to need
engenheiro/a civil	civil engineer
anúncio (m.)	advertisement
Tanto ele como a Ana …	Both he and Ana …
uns anos (m.)	a few years, for a few years (see uses of indefinite article in section 1.3)
tencionar + infinitive	to intend to
casar-se	to marry, to get married
daqui a dois anos	in two years from now
correr	to run, to proceed
se tudo correr bem	if all goes well
voo (m.)	flight
Oxalá …	Hopefully …
(This idiomatic expression derives from the Arabic *Inshallah*, meaning "God willing.")	
nevoeiro (m.)	fog
greve (f.)	strike
desejar	to wish
Adeus.	Goodbye.
Até à vista.	Bye for now. See you.

Practice

Problemas nos Correios

A Joana entra nos Correios para enviar uma encomenda.

JOANA Por favor! Queria enviar esta encomenda.

FUNCIONÁRIO A minha colega no número três está livre. Faça favor!

JOANA Quanto custa enviar esta encomenda para o norte?

FUNCIONÁRIO É o mesmo para todo o país. O preço depende do peso. Também precisa da morada completa.

JOANA Vou ter de telefonar à minha amiga para saber o código postal.
[Joana marca o número, mas não consegue estabelecer ligação.]

JOANA Desculpe, não consigo obter sinal do número que desejo.

FUNCIONÁRIO Não estará impedido?

JOANA Não, a linha parece estar em baixo.

FUNCIONÁRIO Qual é o número que pretende?

JOANA 54-0345.

FUNCIONÁRIO Falta um algarismo. Depois do indicativo 54 tem que ter cinco algarismos. É melhor dirigir-se às informações online para confirmar o número.

JOANA Só preciso de verificar o código postal da minha amiga.

FUNCIONÁRIO Qual é a morada dela?

JOANA Rua do Torto, número dezasseis.

FUNCIONÁRIO Em que cidade?

JOANA Braga.

FUNCIONÁRIO Rua do Porto em Braga...

JOANA Não, do Torto. "T" como em tonta, como eu hoje!

FUNCIONÁRIO Pronto! Já compreendi. Não se aflija!

VOCABULARY

entrar	to go in, to enter
enviar	to send
correios (m.)	post office
encomenda (f.)	package
balcão (m.)	counter
colega	colleague (m. & f.)
é o mesmo	it's the same
o norte	the north
preço (m.)	price
peso (m.)	weight
morada (f.)	address
telefonema (m.),	phone call
chamada (f.) telefónica	
marcar	to dial
ligação (f.)	connection
não consegue	he/she doesn't succeed (from the verb **conseguir**)
obter	to obtain
que desejo	that I want/wish
sinal (m.)	tone, signal
Não estará impedido?	Might it be busy?
a linha (f.) parece estar em baixo	the line appears to be down
que pretende	that you want
falta um algarismo	a digit is missing
depois do indicativo	after the code number
é melhor	it is better
dirigir-se às ...	to contact the ...
Informações	Enquiries
confirmar	to confirm
verificar	to check
pronto	OK
Já compreendi.	I have understood. I've got it.
Não se aflija.	Don't worry.
tonto/a (in Brazil: **bôbo/a**)	idiot

5

PRACTICE EXERCISE

Answer the following questions based on the preceding dialogue:

1 Porque precisa a Joana de ir aos correios?
2 Qual é o número do balcão que está livre?
3 De que depende o custo do envio de uma encomenda?
4 Porque precisa de telefonar à sua amiga?
5 Ela consegue fazer a ligação?
6 Não estará impedido?
7 Qual é o problema com o número da Joana?
8 Qual é o conselho (advice) que a funcionária lhe dá?
9 De que precisa a Joana?
10 Que informação dá a Joana à funcionária para descobrir o código postal?
11 Que respondeu a funcionária?

Week 6

- *the imperfect tense ("was doing," "used to do")*
- *verbs to express "to know," "to play," and "to take"*
- *useful vocabulary for meals*
- *adverbs of place (e.g., "here," "there")*
- *more about personal pronouns: direct and indirect objects and reflexive pronouns ("him," "to him," "himself," etc.)*

6.1 THE IMPERFECT TENSE ("WAS DOING," "USED TO DO")

The imperfect is used to talk about a regular, repeated action or a continuous action in the past. It is the equivalent of "was/were" + present participle or "used to" + infinitive in English—what was happening or used to happen in the past. (Remember that the preterite is used to describe a one-off completed action.)

In Portuguese, the imperfect is a simple (single word) tense. For all verbs ending in **-ar**, the infinitive ending is replaced with **-ava**, etc. For all verbs ending in **-er** and **-ir**, the infinitive ending is replaced with **-ia**, etc. The full conjugations are shown below.

	falar to speak	**comer** to eat	**abrir** to open
eu	fal<u>ava</u>	com<u>ia</u>	abr<u>ia</u>
tu	fal<u>avas</u>	com<u>ias</u>	abr<u>ias</u>
ele, ela, você	fal<u>ava</u>	com<u>ia</u>	abr<u>ia</u>
nós	fal<u>ávamos</u>	com<u>íamos</u>	abr<u>íamos</u>
eles, elas, vocês	fal<u>avam</u>	com<u>iam</u>	abr<u>iam</u>

There are only four exceptions in the second group:
ter ("to have") **tinha, tinhas, tinha, tínhamos, tinham**
vir ("to come") **vinha, vinhas, vinha, vínhamos, vinham**
pôr ("to put") **punha, punhas, punha, púnhamos, punham ser** ("to be") **era, eras, era, éramos, eram**

Here are some examples of the use of the imperfect:

Era uma vez ...
Once upon a time ... ("It used to be a time ...")

Estava ao telefone quando ele entrou.
I was on the phone when he came in.
(**Estava** is in the imperfect, as it describes an ongoing action that took place in the past, whereas **entrou** is in the preterite, as it describes a one-off event.)

Quando era pequena, brincava com as tuas bonecas.
When I was little, I used to play with your dolls.

Ela jogava ténis todas as manhãs.
She used to play tennis every morning. (habitual action)

Ela nunca comia bolos.
She never used to eat cakes. (imperfect)
But
Ela nunca comeu bolos.
She has never eaten cakes. (preterite)

In Portuguese, the imperfect is frequently used in place of the conditional. For example, "I would like to have ..." is very often expressed by **gostava de ter ...** instead of **gostaria** (see section 7.7).

6.2 VERBS FOR "TO KNOW," "TO PLAY," "TO TAKE"

1 In Portuguese, there are two verbs for "to know": **conhecer** ("to be acquainted with") and **saber** ("to have knowledge of," "to know how to").

Não sabia se vinham.
I didn't know whether they were coming.

Conhecia-os bem há muito tempo.
I used to know them well a long time ago.

To express ability (e.g., "Can you swim?"), **saber** is used in Portuguese: **Sabes nadar?** ("Do you know how to swim?"). Using **poder** ("to be able to") would imply permission to do so: **Podes nadar?** ("Are you allowed to swim?") **Não posso nadar.** ("I'm not allowed to swim" or "I'm unable to," due to some physical condition.)

Besides "to know" in the sense of "to be familiar with," **conhecer** also means "to meet" (for the first time):

Conheci-os o ano passado.
I met them last year.
(Note the use of the preterite.)

2 "To play" can be translated in a variety of ways in Portuguese, depending on the context. The verb **brincar** is used to talk about playing with toys, playing with children, or teasing. The verb **jogar** is used for playing games or sports, while **tocar** means to play music or to ring a doorbell. (Coupled with the preposition **em**, **tocar** also means "to touch.") And **desempenhar (um papel)** means "to play (a role)." Here are some examples:

Ela brinca no jardim.
She is playing in the garden.
Não ligues nenhuma, ele está a brincar contigo.
Don't pay any attention, he is teasing you.
Jogo as cartas.
I play cards.
Ela toca guitarra.
She plays the guitar.
O ator desempenhou o papel de Otelo muito bem.
The actor played the part of Othello very well.

3 There are several Portuguese verbs that can convey "to take" in English in different contexts.

tomar   to take (touch, seize, grasp with one's hands)
          to take a bus or a train
          to take a bath
          (also, to have food or drink)

Eu vou tomar um café com leite.
I'm going to have ("take") a coffee with milk.

levar   to take (in the sense of carrying)
             to take (in relation to time)
             idiomatic: to charge (money)

Levo estas malas comigo.
I'm taking these suitcases with me.
É importante levar o tempo necessário.
It is important to take the time necessary.
Quanto me leva (você) por isto?
How much will you charge me for this?

tirar   to take away, out, from
            to take off, remove
            to take photos, a course, an exam, a copy

Ele tirou o casaco.
He took off his coat.
Ela tirou-me a escova do cabelo.
She took away my hairbrush.
(Você) tira muito boas fotografias.
You take very good photos.
But
O avião levanta voo (Brazil: **vôo).**
The plane takes off.

It can be easy to confuse **levar** ("to take") and **trazer** ("to bring") or **ir** ("to go") and **vir** ("to come"). Try to remember that **levar** and **ir** convey movement away from the speaker ("taking," "going"), while **trazer** and **vir** refer to movement toward the speaker ("bringing," "coming"). Thus, rather than "I am coming to your house to bring flowers," in Portuguese you would say:
Vou (I'm going) **a tua casa para levar** (to take) **flores.**

Exercise 1

Translate the following:

1 Quando era criança aprendia tudo mais facilmente.
2 Eu antes comia muito, mas agora não.
3 Íamos todos os dias à praia.
4 Ontem fomos ao campo.
5 Era debaixo desta árvore que eu costumava sentar-me.
6 Que estava (você) a fazer?
7 Eu estava a tomar banho.
8 What time did you have your breakfast?
9 Would you please tell me where the bus stop is?
10 Can you (fam.) play the guitar?
11 It was raining cats and dogs when we went out.
12 He was listening while I was speaking.
13 I was already eating.
14 Last night I had dinner (dined) with my mother-in-law.

6

VOCABULARY 1

aprender	to learn
tudo	everything
facilmente	easily
antes	before
agora não	not now
fomos	we went (preterite of the verb **ir**)
campo (m.)	country, countryside, field
debaixo	under, underneath
costumava	I used to, I was in the habit of
sentar-se	to sit down
a tomar banho	to take a bath
paragem (f.) do autocarro (m.)	bus stop
É verdade?	Is it true?
chover a cântaros/potes	to rain (cats and dogs)
enquanto	while
sair	to go out, to leave
ouvir	to listen
sogro/a	father/mother-in-law

6.3 MEALS (**REFEIÇÕES**)

o pequeno-almoço breakfast
(in Brazil: **café da manhã**)
o almoço lunch
o lanche tea time, mid-afternoon snack; also **a merenda**
o jantar dinner
a ceia supper (light meal taken in the evening)

and their respective verbs:

tomar o pequeno-almoço to have breakfast
almoçar to have lunch
lanchar to have a snack
jantar to have dinner

6.4 ADVERBS OF PLACE ("HERE," "THERE")

aqui, cá	here (practically no difference between these, but **cá** tends to be used more idiomatically)
ali	there (for something you can see)
lá	there (you don't have to be able to see it, it is also employed in a more abstract sense)
aí	there (something close to the person you're speaking to; it can also mean "somewhere there")
acolá	there (further than **ali**: "over there," "yonder")

Some examples:
Estou aqui há muito tempo.
I have been here for a long time.
Cá estou a escrever-te ...
Here I am, writing to you ...
Venha cá! (also: **Venha aqui!**)
Come here!
O meu irmão está ali.
My brother is there. (pointing to the place)
Como estava o tempo lá?
How was the weather there? (speaking of a place away from both speakers)

Lá vai ela!
There she goes!

Como está o tempo aí?
How is the weather there? (when calling or writing to a
friend about the place where she/he is now)

Onde estão as minhas luvas?
Where are my gloves?
[Your friend in the next room might reply:]
Estão aí.
They are around somewhere.

Vejo uma águia acolá, naquela montanha.
I see an eagle over there, on that mountain.

Note that **aqui**, **ali**, **aí**, and **lá**, often combined with a
preposition, can be used in expressions of time:

Daqui a 15 dias.
In two weeks' time.
Dali, ele foi para Macau.
From there, he went to Macau.
Já lá vão cinco anos!
Five years have gone by!

When speaking outside the door of the person you are
talking to:

Nunca mais sais daí?
Aren't you ever going to come out of there?

Exercise 2

1 O avião levou 6 horas para lá chegar.

2 Hoje não quero brincar com as crianças; prefiro jogar xadrez.

3 Ele vem cá muitas vezes.

4 Ela foi para Nova Iorque e dali foi para o México.

5 Senhor doutor, quantos comprimidos (pills/tablets) tenho de tomar?

6 Tive de (I had to) tirar dinheiro da minha conta-depósito.

7 How is the weather there? (speaking to someone on the phone)

8 Your gloves are around somewhere.

9 The bus stop is there.

10 Here I am!

11 I see a boat over there. (far away)

12 Your keys are here.

6.5 MORE ON PERSONAL PRONOUNS

Below are the direct object pronouns (e.g., "him"/"her"), the indirect object pronouns (e.g., "to him"/"her"), and the reflexive pronouns (e.g., "himself"/"herself"):

direct object	indirect object	reflexive
me me	**me** to/for me	**me** myself
te you (fam.)	**te** to/for you	**te** yourself
o you (form.)	**lhe** to/for you	**se** yourself
a you (form.)	**lhe** to/for you	**se** yourself
o him, it	**lhe** to/for him, it	**se** himself, itself
a her, it	**lhe** to/for her, it	**se** herself, itself
nos us	**nos** to/for us	**nos** ourselves
vos you (pl.)	**vos** to/for you	**vos** yourselves
os you (pl. form.)	**lhes** to/for you	**se** yourselves
as you (pl. form.)	**lhes** to/for you	**se** yourselves
os them	**lhes** to/for them	**se** themselves
as them	**lhes** to/for them	**se** themselves

COMBINED FORMS

When one of the direct object pronouns **o**, **a**, **os**, or **as** and an indirect object pronoun occur together—as in the sentence "he gave it to me"—they form compound words. The indirect object pronoun always comes first:

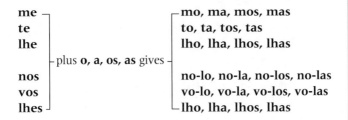

me ⎤
te ⎥
lhe ⎥
⎬ plus **o, a, os, as** gives ⎨
nos ⎥
vos ⎥
lhes ⎦

⎡ **mo, ma, mos, mas**
to, ta, tos, tas
lho, lha, lhos, lhas

no-lo, no-la, no-los, no-las
vo-lo, vo-la, vo-los, vo-las
⎣ **lho, lha, lhos, lhas**

For example:

Dou-lhe a minha morada. I give my address to him.
Dou-lha. I give it (f.) to him. (i.e., **morada**)

Note that before another pronoun, the **-s** of **nos** and **vos** is omitted and replaced by a hyphen. However, these forms (**no-lo**, **vo-lo**, etc.) are seldom used in conversation.

WORD ORDER

In affirmative main sentences, the object pronouns follow the verb and are joined to it by a hyphen. But there are certain circumstances in which they precede the verb:

1 In negative sentences

Não o vejo. I don't see him/it.

2 In questions

Porque não nos fala? Why don't you speak to us?

3 After some prepositions, conjunctions, and adverbs

Sempre me detestou.
He/she/you (formal) always hated me.

Depois de lhe dar a receita ...
After giving him/her/you (formal) the prescription ...
Antes que me esqueça ...
Before I forget ...
Eles mal me falam.
They hardly speak to me.

Note that the verb **esquecer-se** ("to forget") is reflexive in Portuguese.

PRONOUNS AFTER VERBS ENDING IN -R, -S, AND -Z

When a verb ends in **-r**, **-s**, or **-z**, this letter is dropped before the pronouns **o**, **a**, **os**, and **as**. The letter **l-** is then prefixed to the pronoun, which is joined to the verb by a hyphen. The verb is stressed, so an acute accent is added over the letter **a** or a circumflex accent over **e** and **o**. Here are some examples of this:

Eu quero ver o António.
I want to see Anthony.
Eu quero vê-lo.
I want to see him.

Eu desejo comprar uvas.
I want to buy some grapes.
Eu desejo comprá-las.
I want to buy them.

Ela faz cestos.
She makes baskets.
Ela fá-los.
She makes them.

Nós vemos a sua amiga muitas vezes.
We often see your friend.
Nós vemo-la muitas vezes.
We often see her.

PRONOUNS AFTER VERBS ENDING IN -M, -ÃO, AND -ÕE

When the pronouns **o**, **a**, **os**, and **as** come immediately after a verb ending in **-m**, **-ão**, or **-õe**, the letter **n-** is prefixed to the pronoun, resulting in the forms **no**, **na**, **nos**, and **nas**, which are then joined to the verb by a hyphen, as shown in the following examples:

Eles dão aulas ao ar livre.
They give lessons in the open air.
Eles dão-nas ao ar livre.
They give them in the open air.

Elas viram o irmão da Maria.
They saw Maria's brother.
Elas viram-no.
They saw him.

Ela põe a mesa.
She sets the table.
Ela põe-na.
She sets it.

But the rule governing the position of object pronouns in negative sentences and questions still applies:

Elas não o viram.
They didn't see him.
Ela a põe?
Is she setting it? (i.e., **a mesa**)

WORD ORDER IN BRAZIL

In Brazilian Portuguese, the object pronouns nearly always come before the verb. Therefore, in Brazil, the word order in the above examples would be:

Eles as dão ao ar livre.
Elas o viram.
Ela a põe.

In Brazil, the reflexive pronoun also comes before the verb. For example:

Eu me sinto cansada. I (f.) feel tired.
But in Portugal:
Eu sinto-me cansada.

OBJECT PRONOUNS AFTER PREPOSITIONS

All the preceding information applies to object pronouns used with verbs. If a pronoun is used after a preposition, it takes a different form. These are called disjunctive (or stressed) pronouns and are employed in the case of verb + preposition (such as **gostar de**).
The disjunctive pronouns are:

mim	me
ti	you (sing. familiar)
si,* você,	you (sing. formal)
o senhor,	
a senhora	
ele	him
ela	her
nós	us
vós, vocês	you (plural fam. & formal)
os senhores,	you (plural, most formal)
as senhoras	
eles, elas	them

* **si** can also mean himself/herself, themselves.
Ele fala de si para si. He is speaking to himself.

Here are some examples of the use of these pronouns after prepositions:

Este livro é para mim.
This book is for me.
Ele gosta de ti.
He likes you (familiar).
Gosto dela.
I like her.

Eu paguei por ela.
I paid for her.
Eu acredito em si.
I believe in you (formal).

These pronouns are especially useful for avoiding the ambiguity that can arise from the combined forms. For this reason, the disjunctive forms are much more common in speech. For example:

Dei-lhes o lápis. I gave them the pencil.
becomes
Dei-o a eles. I gave it to them. (rather than **Dei-lho.**)

An exception: **com**

The preposition **com**, meaning "with," combines with the pronouns **mim**, **ti**, **si**, **nós**, and **vós**, resulting in the following special forms:

singular
com + mim = comigo	with me
com + ti = contigo	with you (familiar)
com + si = consigo	with you (formal) Also: with himself/herself/oneself

But note:
com ele, com ela   with him, with her

plural
com + nós = connosco	with us
(or **conosco** in Brazil)	
com + vós = convosco	with you
com eles, com elas	with them (m. & f.)

When addressing someone politely, "with you" can also be **com o senhor**, **com os senhores**, **com você**, etc.

There are a number of adverbs and prepositions that are commonly followed by these pronouns.

atrás de	behind
perto de	near
longe de	far from
em frente de	in front of
em cima de	on, on top of
por baixo de	under, below
contra	against
sem	without
entre	between, among
antes de	before
depois de	after

OMISSION OF THE THIRD-PERSON PRONOUN

When the third-person pronoun corresponds to an inanimate object or an abstract idea and comes at the end of a phrase or sentence, it is often omitted, as in the following examples:

(Você) viu o filme *E tudo o vento levou*?
Have you seen the film *Gone with the Wind*?
Sim, vi.
Yes, I've seen it.

O senhor come carne?
Do you eat meat?
Sim, como.
Yes, I eat it.

Gosta de Portugal?
Do you like Portugal?
Sim, gosto.
Yes, I like it.

Vocês beberam o vinho?
Did you drink the wine?
Sim, bebemos.
Yes, we drank it.

6

Exercise 3

Translate the following:

1 Dê-lhe os meus cumprimentos.
2 Ela telefonou-me ontem à noite.
3 Viu-o na semana passada.
4 Não as conheço bem.
5 Eles visitam-nos todos os anos.
6 Queremos vê-lo.
7 Vou ajudá-la.
8 Vocês ajudam-no muito.
9 Ele não quer as maçãs, mas eu vou dar-lhas.
10 Você mora perto de mim.
11 Não como sem você.
12 Venha comigo agora tomar um café e depois eu vou consigo ao cabeleireiro.
13 Os cães estão connosco, mas os gatos estão com elas.
14 Quem lho disse?

6

VOCABULARY 2

dê	give (polite imperative of **dar**)
cumprimentos	regards, best regards
telefonar	to call (on the phone)
viu	he/she sees (preterite of **ver**)
conhecer	to know (to be acquainted with)
visitar	to visit
querer	to want
ajudar	to help
depois	after, afterward, then
cabeleireiro/a	hairdresser
cão (m.) (pl. cães)	dog (see section 5.2)
gato (m.)	cat
disse	I, you, he/she said (preterite of **dizer**)

Exercise 4

Translate the following:

1 Show us what you (polite sing.) found.
2 Go (familiar sing.) and look for her.
3 Are these flowers for me?
4 Before I forget, I have to tell you (pl.).
5 He waited for us.
6 Come (polite sing.) with me.
7 There are no secrets between us.
8 I am counting on you (familiar sing.).
9 He did not lend it to me.
10 They help him.
11 My mother didn't call me (on the phone).
12 I don't need him.
13 I called him, but he didn't hear me.
14 I saw them (m.) last week.
15 He is going to see her.

VOCABULARY 3

mostrar	to show
procurar	to look for (in Brazil: **buscar**)
esperar	to wait
segredo (m.)	secret
contar com	to count on, to count with
emprestar	to lend
ajudar	to help
telefonar	to call (on the phone)
precisar de	to need
chamar	to call
ouvir	to hear
vi	I saw (preterite of **ver**)

Practice

DIALOGUE

Um aniversário/A birthday

ANTÓNIA   O domingo passado foi o dia dos anos
do meu sogro. Foi uma grande festa.
Estava lá, praticamente, toda a família:
os sobrinhos americanos do meu sogro,
a tia do meu marido que veio do Brasil,
os meus cunhados e cunhadas e os netos
todos dos meus sogros que, ao todo,
são nove.

MIGUEL   Meu Deus, tanta gente! Deve ter sido
um pandemónio com essa malta toda.

ANTÓNIA   Não, nem por isso. Estava tudo muito
bem organizado. Como estava calor,
mandámos os mais novos para a piscina e
pusemos a gente mais velha a jogar xadrez.
Nós, os anfitriões, estávamos encarregues
de todos os preparativos, enquanto os
convidados bebiam e discutiam os últimos
acontecimentos.

MIGUEL   Quantos anos fez o teu sogro?

ANTÓNIA   Fez sessenta e cinco anos.

MIGUEL   Não parece, está muito bem conservado.
Quando o vires, dá-lhe os meus sinceros
parabéns. Tem graça que a minha enteada
também fez anos no dia vinte e oito.
Fez dezoito anos. Mas com essa não
tivemos problema. Ela foi para a discoteca
com os amigos e nós só pagámos a conta.
Voltando ao assunto da tua festa,
que comeram?

ANTÓNIA   Bem, para o almoço tivemos saladas,
ovos, queijo, camarões, azeitonas e fruta—
muitas uvas e melões e também melancia.
Depois da sesta lanchámos: chá, torradas,
biscoitos feitos em casa e o bolo dos anos
com as velas. E por volta das oito jantámos.

6

Era leitão assado no espeto—no jardim, é claro—ervilhas, batatas e outros legumes. Para sobremesa tivemos uma grande variedade de pudins. O vinho era do melhor, das adegas do meu cunhado e, naturalmente, não faltava o champanhe.

VOCABULARY

dia (m.) dos anos	birthday
uma grande festa (f.)	a big party
ao todo	in all
tanta gente (f.)	so many people
deve ter sido	it must have been
essa malta (f.) toda	all that crowd (colloquial)
nem por isso	not really, not too bad
quantos anos fez ...	how old was ...
não parece	he doesn't look it, he doesn't seem ...
bem conservado	well preserved
quando o/a vir	when you see him/her
Parabéns!	Happy birthday! (also Congratulations!)
tem graça	how funny, it's funny, what a coincidence
mas com essa	but with that one (f.), with her
voltando ao assunto	coming back to the subject
e por volta das oito	and around eight o'clock
era do melhor	it was of the best
não faltava	we were not short of, there was no lack of
sogro/a	father/mother-in-law
praticamente	practically
toda a família (f.)	the whole family
sobrinho/a	nephew/niece
cunhado/a	brother/sister-in-law
neto/a	grandson/granddaughter
pandemónio (m.)	pandemonium
(in Brazil: **pandemônio**)	
organizado	organized (past participle of **organizar**)

mandámos	we sent (preterite of **mandar**)
os mais novos	the younger ones
pusemos	we put, we set (preterite of irregular verb **pôr**)
mais velho	older
xadrez (m.)	chess
anfitrião/anfitriã	host
encarregado	in charge
enquanto	while
convidado/a	guest
discutir	to discuss
últimos acontecimentos (m.)	latest events
Quantos anos fez?	How old were you (polite)? How old was he/she?
dá-lhe	give him (familiar imperative of **dar**)
enteado/a	stepson/stepdaughter
tivemos	we had (preterite of **ter**)
foi	he/she/it went, he/she/it was
pagar	to pay
ovo (m.)	egg
queijo (m.)	cheese
camarão (m.)	shrimp (pl. **camarões**)
azeitona (f.)	olive
uva (f.)	grape
melão (m.)	melon (pl. **melões**)
melancia (f.)	watermelon
sesta (f.)	nap
chá (m.)	tea
torrada (f.)	toast
biscoito (m.)	cookie
feito em casa	homemade (past part. of **fazer**)
vela (f.)	candle
leitão (m.)	suckling pig
assado	roasted
espeto (m.)	spit
jardim (m.)	garden
é claro	of course, naturally
ervilha (f.)	pea
batata (f.)	potato

6

outros	others
legume (m.)	vegetable
sobremesa (f.)	dessert
variedade (f.)	variety
pudim (m.)	pudding (pl. **pudins**)
vinho (m.)	wine
adega (f.)	wine cellar

PRACTICE EXERCISE

Answer the following questions based on the preceding dialogue:

1 Quem são as protagonistas deste diálogo?
2 De quem falam?
3 O que aconteceu (what happened) no domingo?
4 Havia pouca gente?
5 Descreva a família.
6 Que faziam os jovens?
7 Quantos anos fez o sogro?
8 Ele parece muito velho?
9 Quem mais fez anos no dia vinte e oito?
10 Ela teve uma grande festa?
11 Quem pagou a conta?
12 Descreva o que comeram na festa dos anos—ao almoço, lanche e jantar.

Week 7

- *"either … or," "neither … nor"*
- *negatives such as "nothing," "never," etc.*
- *how to use* **já**
- *indefinite adjectives and pronouns (e.g., "certain," "few," "all," "some," etc.)*
- *making comparisons ("more/less than," "as … as," etc.)*
- *expressions for love and hate*
- *the future and conditional ("I will …," "I would …")*

7.1 "EITHER … OR," "NEITHER … NOR"

The Portuguese word for "or" is **ou**, and to say "either … or," it is simply repeated: **ou … ou**. "Neither … nor" is **nem … nem**.

Quem manda aqui, sou eu ou você?
Who's in charge here (lit. "Who gives orders here"), is it me or you?

Nem eu nem a minha mulher nem os meus filhos gostamos de ar condicionado.
Neither I nor my wife nor my children like air-conditioning.

"Neither one nor the other" is translated by **nem um nem outro** (m.)/**nem uma nem outra** (f.).

Two things to note in the sentences above that differ from English: one is that the pronoun **eu** comes first (**eu e a minha mulher** instead of "my wife and I"). The other is that in Portuguese, **nem** can be repeated as many times as necessary.

nem and **nem mesmo** translate as "not even." For example:

Nem quero sonhar uma coisa dessas.
I don't even want to think (lit. "dream") of such a thing.
Nem mesmo se o senhor me pagasse.
Not even if you paid me.

Nem is sometimes used in place of **não**. For example:

Nem me diga ... You don't say ..., Don't tell me ...
Nem por isso. Not really.

7.2 MORE NEGATIVES ("NOTHING," "NEVER," "NO ONE," ETC.)

nada nothing
nunca never
jamais never
nunca ... mais never again
já não no longer, not anymore
ainda não not yet
ninguém no one
nenhum (m.), nenhuma (f.),
  nenhuns (m. pl.), nenhumas (f. pl.) none, not any

Não conheço ninguém aqui.
I don't know anyone here.
Ele não tem nenhuma ideia.
He doesn't have any idea.
Nunca mais compro sapatos de salto alto.
Never again will I buy high-heeled shoes.
Eles não têm nada.
They have nothing.
Nunca o vi na minha vida.
I have never seen him in my life.
Ele já não mora no Porto.
He no longer lives in Porto.
Hoje ainda não comi.
I haven't eaten yet today.

Be aware of another meaning of **já não**. For example:

Já não o via há tantos anos!
I hadn't seen him for so many years!

Note that unlike in English, double negatives are
frequently used in Portuguese.

The word **já** means "already" when used with a past-tense verb, but it appears much more frequently in Portuguese than in English. For example:

Já comeu?/Já comeste?
Have you eaten? (polite/familiar)

When **já** is used with a verb in the present tense, it means "soon" (also often omitted in English):

Eu já vou.
I'm coming.

Here are some other uses or meanings:

já, já (in Brazil)
right away (**imediatamente** in Portugal)
desde já
from this moment on
Já não quero isso.
I don't want that anymore.
Já agora aproveito para comprar ...
While I'm at it, I'll (take the opportunity to) buy ...
Já que a sorte a trouxe aqui ...
Since luck brought you here ...

já can also mean "ever" when used in a question. For example:

Já viste uma beleza destas?
Have you ever seen a beauty like this?

7

Exercise 1

Translate the following:

1 (Você) quer tomar chá ou café?
2 Nem quero chá nem café. Prefiro um sumo de laranja.
3 Ou vou ao cinema ou fico em casa, a ver televisão, ainda não tenho a certeza.
4 Nunca vi uma exposição tão bem organizada.
5 Ele não tem escrúpulos nenhuns.
6 Nunca mais compro aparelhos elétricos em segunda mão.
7 (Você) não tem nada a ver com isso.
8 Aqui ninguém fala inglês.
9 Eu não sei nada.
10 Não fomos a lado nenhum.

Exercise 2

Translate the following:

1 Have you (familiar sing.) ever eaten bacalhau à Gomes de Sá?
2 No one told me that.
3 While I'm here, I'll also send this email.
4 We have never seen him.
5 I don't have any (f.).
6 I haven't seen this film yet.
7 She no longer likes him.
8 He is bringing the file soon.
9 As she has apologized ("asked pardon"), I consider the matter closed.
10 They (f.) never went anywhere.

VOCABULARY 1

café (m.)	coffee
sumo (m.)	orange juice
de laranja (f.) (in Brazil: **suco de laranja**)	
ficar	to stay, to remain
ainda	yet, still
não tenho a certeza	I'm not sure
(in Brazil: **não estou certo/a**)	
exposição (f.)	exhibition
escrúpulos (m.)	scruples
aparelho (m.) elétrico	electrical appliance
segunda mão (f.)	secondhand
não ter nada a ver com ...	to have nothing to do with
sei	I know (present tense of **saber**)
fomos	we went (preterite of **ir**)
lado nenhum	nowhere, not anywhere
bacalhau (m.) à Gomes de Sá	dried cod (**bacalhau**) fried with onions, potatoes, etc.
filme (m.)	film
pedir desculpa	to apologize
ficha (f.)	file, form
o assunto (m.) está encerrado/acabou	the matter is closed

7.4 "CERTAIN," "FEW," "ALL," "SOME," ETC.

Note the feminine and plural forms of these indefinite adjectives and pronouns:

certo, certa, certos, certas certain
outro, outra, outros, outras other
pouco, pouca little, **poucos, poucas** few
todo, toda, todos, todas every, all
algum, alguma, alguns, algumas some, any
um, uma, uns, umas one, some
(often used in place of **algum, algumas**)

tudo everything
tanto, tanta so much, **tantos, tantas** so many
tal, tais such
qualquer, quaisquer any, whatever (of a choice)
ambos, ambas both
alguém someone, anyone
cada each

7.5 MAKING COMPARISONS

The comparative is usually formed using **mais** ("more") or **menos** ("less") + adjective + **do que** (or merely **que**):

Ela é mais bonita do que a irmã.
or **Ela é mais bonita que a irmã.**
She is prettier than her sister.
Ela tem menos dinheiro do que eu.
She has less money than I do.

tão … como as … as
Ela é tão rica como eu. She is as rich as I am.

tanto/a … como, tantos/as … como
as much/many … as
Tem tanto dinheiro como eu.
She has as much money as I do.

In Brazil, "as … as" is **tão … quanto** (or **tanto … quanto**, which is also occasionally used in Portugal).

THE SUPERLATIVE
The superlative is formed by putting the articles **o**, **a**, **os**, and **as** before **mais** ("more") or **menos** ("less"), turning them into "the most," "the least." For example:

Ela é a mais bonita. She is the prettiest.

The intensifier "very" can be rendered by **muito**:
Ela é muito bonita. She is very pretty.

And the superlative intensifier "extremely" is conveyed by adding **-íssimo** to the adjective after dropping the final vowel. For example:

lindo (beautiful) > **lindíssimo** (extremely beautiful)
barato (cheap) > **baratíssimo** (extremely cheap)

Some superlatives are irregular:

fácil (easy) > **facílimo**
rico (rich) > **riquíssimo**
feliz (happy) > **felicíssimo**
amável (kind) > **amabilíssimo**
pobre (poor) > **paupérrimo**

And some adjectives/adverbs have irregular comparatives:

bom, boa, bem good, well	**melhor** better	**o melhor** the best	**ótimo** super
mau, má, mal bad, badly	**pior** worse	**o pior** the worst	**péssimo** extremely bad
grande large, big	**maior** larger	**o maior** the largest	**máximo** maximum
pequeno small, little	**mais pequeno** *or* **menor**	**o mais pequeno** *or* **o menor**	**mínimo** minimum
alto tall, high, loud	**mais alto** *or* **superior**	**o mais alto**	**supremo**
baixo low, short	**mais baixo** *or* **inferior**	**o mais baixo**	**ínfimo**
muito very	**mais** more/-er	**o mais** the most/-est	
pouco little/few	**menos** less	**o menos** *or* **o mínimo** the least	

Ele é a autoridade suprema. He is the highest authority.
O tempo está péssimo. The weather is awful.
Uma ótima ideia. A super idea.
Ela é a mais linda das irmãs. She is the prettiest of the sisters.

Adverbs ending in -ly in English are generally formed in Portuguese by adding **-mente** to the feminine singular of the adjective. For example:

raro > **raramente** rarely
absoluto > **absolutamente** absolutely
fácil > **facilmente** easily

When two or more adverbs of this type come together, **-mente** is added only to the last one. For example:

Ele falou clara e vagarosamente.
He spoke clearly and slowly.

Exercise 3

Translate the following:

1 Does anyone speak English here?
2 Did you ("o senhor") ask me for a spoon or a knife?
3 Neither. I asked you for a fork.
4 He has some hope (hopes).
5 Each to his/her own taste.
6 Everything is very expensive.
7 Do you (pl.) have any English magazines?
8 They are both writers.
9 The dinner was awful.
10 My aunt is very ill.
11 He is the richest man in the world.
12 I have good news for you (familiar).
13 She is as happy as I am.
14 Camões was the greatest Portuguese poet.

VOCABULARY 2

pedir	to ask for
colher (f.)	spoon
faca (f.)	knife
nem um(a) nem outro/a	neither (one nor the other)
garfo (m.)	fork
esperança (f.)	hope
cada qual	each (one)
gosto (m.)	taste
caro	expensive
revista (f.)	magazine
escritor/ escritora	writer
do mundo	in the world
notícias (f.)	news
para ti/si	for you (familiar/polite)
(in Brazil: **para você**)	

7.6 EXPRESSIONS FOR "LOVE" AND "HATE"

The verb **amar** is less commonly used in Portuguese than in English. It is reserved for deep feelings, for example, between a couple: **Amo-te** ("I love you"). In most other situations, the Portuguese tend to use **gostar muito de ...** or **adorar**:

Gosto muito de ti.
I like you very much.
Adoro cantar.
I love singing.

By the same token, **odiar** ("to hate") is a very strong word. In most cases, the verb **detestar** is used:

Adoro a Inglaterra, mas detesto o frio e a chuva.
I love England, but I hate the cold and the rain.

In the text that follows, you'll see an example of this cultural difference between Portuguese and English.

Quando vim a Londres, pela primeira vez, ouvi o condutor do autocarro chamar-me "amor" quando me pedia que bilhete eu queria. Fiquei visivelmente chocada e corei até às raízes do cabelo.

condutor(a) do autocarro	bus driver
corar	to blush
raiz (f.)	root
cabelo (m. sing.)	hair

7.7 THE FUTURE AND CONDITIONAL ("I WILL ...," "I WOULD ...")

The future (e.g., "I will speak") and the conditional (e.g., "I would speak") are simple (single word) verb forms in Portuguese. To form them, the conjugation endings are simply added to the infinitive. Here are the endings for **-ar, -er,** and **-ir** verbs.

	falar	**ter**	**ir**
	to speak	to have	to go
Future tense			
eu	**falarei**	**terei**	**irei**
tu	**falarás**	**terás**	**irás**
ele, ela, você	**falará**	**terá**	**irá**
nós	**falaremos**	**teremos**	**iremos**
eles, elas, vocês	**falarão**	**terão**	**irão**
Conditional			
eu	**falaria**	**teria**	**iria**
tu	**falarias**	**terias**	**irias**
ele, ela, você	**falaria**	**teria**	**iria**
nós	**falaríamos**	**teríamos**	**iríamos**
eles, elas, vocês	**falariam**	**teriam**	**iriam**

There are only three exceptions to this: **dizer** ("to say"), **fazer** ("to make," "to do"), and **trazer** ("to bring"). While the conjugation endings for these three verbs follow the pattern just described, the infinitive to which the endings are added is modified:

dizer *becomes*:
direi, -ás, -á, -emos, -ão (future)
diria, -ias, -ia, -íamos, -iam (conditional)

fazer *becomes*:
farei, -ás, -á, -emos, -ão (future)
faria, -ias, -ia, -íamos, -iam (conditional)

trazer *becomes*:
trarei, -ás, -á, -emos, -ão (future)
traria, -ias, -ia, -íamos, -iam (conditional)

When the future and conditional are followed by an object pronoun, the pronoun is inserted between the stem—that is, the infinitive—and the ending. For example:

Dar-lhe-ei ... I will give him ... (not **Darei-lhe ...**)
Eu far-lho-ia. I would do it for you.
Eles falar-me-ão. They will speak to me.

Apart from this, the rules governing the formation and position of pronouns apply to the future and conditional in exactly the same way as explained in section 6.5.

1 The pronouns precede the verb in negative sentences and questions and after certain adverbs, prepositions, and conjunctions. For example:

Eles não me falarão. They will not speak to me.

2 The final **-r** of the infinitive is dropped before third-person pronouns, and an accent (acute or circumflex) is placed over the final vowel to indicate that it should be stressed, as if the **-r** were still present.

For example:

Fá-lo-ei. I will do it.
Eles comê-lo-ão. They will eat it.

OTHER WAYS OF EXPRESSING THE FUTURE

1 The present tense

In Portuguese, especially conversationally, the present tense is frequently used to express a future intention or action. For example:

Saio amanhã. I'll go out tomorrow.
(I'm going out tomorrow.)

2 Use of **ir** + infinitive

Just as in English, it is possible and common in Portuguese to use the present tense of **ir** ("to go") with an infinitive to express future intention. For example:

Vou sair amanhã. I'm going to go out tomorrow.

3 Use of **haver de** + infinitive

The present tense of **haver** + **de** + infinitive is another method of expressing a strong intention to perform a future action. For example:

(Você) há-de aprender português.
You will learn Portuguese.

For the present tense of **haver**, see section 1.7.

IDIOMATIC USES OF THE FUTURE AND CONDITIONAL

1 In Portuguese, the future and conditional can be used to express the idea of "approximately." In a situation pertaining to the present, the future tense is used, and in a situation pertaining to the past, the conditional is used. For example:

O nosso professor terá uns cinquenta anos.
Our teacher is about fifty years old.
Seriam cinco horas quando ele entrou.
It was about five o'clock when he came in.

2 It is possible to use the future and conditional to convey uncertainty in situations conveyed by the English expression "to wonder whether … ." For example:

Será esta a rua que procuramos?
I wonder whether this is the street we are looking for?
(In Brazil, instead of **procuramos**, you would use **buscamos**.)

Seria ele culpado?
I wonder whether he was guilty?

As shown in the preceding examples, the future tense is used to refer to present circumstances and the conditional to the past.

Note also that the imperfect tense can be used as a substitute for the conditional when the meaning is "I would," etc. For example:

Gostava de ir ao Brasil. = Gostaria de ir ao Brasil.
I would like to go to Brazil.

Exercise 4

Translate the following:

1 When will you (polite) write to him?
2 He has to work a lot.
3 We won't take it.
4 I'll begin my story.
5 Who will win?
6 We will arrive (in the) next month.
7 I wonder if it was true?
8 Eu diria que ele está a mentir.
9 Não me esquecerei de ti.
10 Faria tudo por ela.
11 Eles dar-lhe-ão a minha nova morada.
12 Hei de ir ao Japão.
13 Tenho de ir ao dentista.
14 Será muito caro?

VOCABULARY 3

escrever	to write
muito	a lot
começar	to begin
ganhar	to win
chegar	to arrive
verdade (f.)	truth
mentir	to lie
novo	new
esquecer-se	to forget
Japão	Japan
dentista	dentist (m. & f.)
caro	expensive

7

Um lugar ao sol / A place in the sun

MARIA Ando à procura de casa no Algarve, mas não encontro nada em conta. Devia ter comprado há anos quando o Algarve ainda não era tão conhecido no estrangeiro.

CARLOS Já procuraste nas listas imobiliárias *online*?

MARIA Sim, mas ainda não encontrei nada de jeito. É sempre a mesma história: as casas de que gosto são caras demais e aquelas que são baratas precisam de muitas obras e são muito longe do mar. Quanto aos apartamentos, fazem-me lembrar caixas de fósforos.

CARLOS És muito exigente. Já sabes que se queres coisa boa tens de pagar, especialmente num sítio como o Algarve.

MARIA Sim, já sei; no entanto, continuarei a tentar. Ainda tenho esperanças de arranjar uma casinha de pescadores à beira-mar com um pequeno jardim com três ou quatro quartos, sala, casa de jantar, cozinha e casa de banho com chuveiro, e que não seja muito cara.

CARLOS É tudo? Quando encontrares essa raridade, vê lá se arranjas duas; eu até te pagaria uma comissão com muito prazer.

7

VOCABULARY 4

à procura de	in search of
(In Portuguese there are a number of nouns deriving from verbs—in this case, **procurar** "to look for")	
em conta	reasonably priced
Devia ter comprado há anos.	I should have bought (something) years ago.
tão conhecido	so well known
caro demais (or: **demasiado caro**)	too expensive
quanto a …	as for …
fazem-me lembrar …	they remind me of … (lit. "they make me remember")
muito exigente	very demanding, hard to please
Já sabes.	You know. (familiar)
Já sei.	I know. (I am well aware.)
no entanto	nevertheless
Ainda tenho esperanças.	I still have hopes.
casinha* (f.) de pescadores	a little fishermen's cottage (diminutive of **casa**)
e que não seja muito cara	and that isn't too expensive
(The use of the subjunctive is explained in section 9.2.)	
É tudo?	Is that all?
Vê lá se arranjas duas.	See if you can get two.
(**lá** is often used in an abstract sense colloquially, much as the English saying "Look here.")	
E eu até te pagaria.	I would even pay you.
(**até**, meaning "until," means "even" in this context.)	
encontrar	to find, to meet
no estrangeiro	abroad
estrangeiro/a	foreigner
Já procuraste …?	Have you looked …?
lista (f.) imobiliária	property listings
jeito (m.)	way, manner
resposta (f.)	reply, answer
história (f.)	story, history
barato	cheap

7

obra (f.)	repairs (to house), construction (lit. "work," "opus")
caixa (f.) de fósforos	a box of matches
se	if, whether
querer	to want
coisa (f.) boa	a good thing
sítio (m.)	place
tentar	to try, to attempt
beira-mar	by the sea
mar (m.)	sea
quarto (m.)	bedroom
sala (f.) (de visitas)	living room
casa (f.) de jantar	dining room
cozinha (f.)	kitchen
chuveiro (m.)	shower
comissão (f.)	commission

* The diminutive suffixes **-inho/a**, **-zinho/a**, **-zito/a**, and **-ito/a** are often used in Portuguese, denoting smallness, affection, or pity. For example, you may find **favor** changed to **favorzinho** and **obrigada** changed to **obrigadinha**.

7

Practice

For help with some of the vocabulary in this dialogue, refer to the section "Clothes and colors," p.219.

Um senhor muito chato entra numa loja …

EMPREGADA   Bom dia. Faz favor?

CLIENTE   Bom dia, desejo comprar uma gravata que vi na montra.

EMPREGADA   Sim senhor. Pode descrever-me a gravata que viu, se faz favor.

CLIENTE   Bem, creio que é às riscas. Talvez não. Parece-me que a que eu vi tinha pintinhas.

EMPREGADA   Uma grande diferença!

CLIENTE   Bem, a diferença está na cor.

EMPREGADA   E de que cor era a gravata que viu?

CLIENTE   Julgo que era azul, mas não tenho a certeza. Em todo o caso, eu não gosto de azul; prefiro encarnado, da cor do Benfica.

EMPREGADA   Tenho aqui uma encarnada, às pintinhas que veio da Itália.

CLIENTE   Não quero nada da Itália. De qualquer outro país menos da Itália.

EMPREGADA   Então porquê?

CLIENTE   Então a senhora não sabe que eles nos venceram no futebol?

EMPREGADA   O que tem a ver isso com a gravata? E a propósito de gravata. Tenho aqui uma de xadrez que veio da Inglaterra.

CLIENTE   Não gosto; pareço um homem que vai tocar a gaita de foles. De qualquer modo, minha senhora, eu prefiro comprar coisas portuguesas. Haja patriotismo!

EMPREGADA   Há aqui alguma coisa que lhe agrade?

CLIENTE   Não, não vejo nada.

EMPREGADA   O senhor é muito esquisito.

CLIENTE   Pois sou; mas não sou malcriado.

EMPREGADA   [entredentes] Mas é chato. [em voz alta] Tenho aqui uma verde e encarnada, muito bonita. Ficava-lhe bem.

CLIENTE   E eu vou andar com a bandeira portuguesa ao pescoço?

EMPREGADA [já irritada] Mas afinal, o que é que o senhor deseja?

CLIENTE Nada. E agora que a chuva já passou vou-me embora. Para a próxima, vou escolher uma camisa.

EMPREGADA As nossas camisas não são nada boas. Vá a outra loja.

VOCABULARY

chato/a	(slang) (n.): a nuisance; (adj.): boring, tiresome
montra (f.)	shop window
descrever	to describe
que viu	that he/she/you (polite) saw (preterite of **ver**)
creio que é às riscas	I believe that it has stripes
talvez não	maybe (perhaps)
creio que	
parece-me que	I think that …, it seems to me
julgo que	that … , I believe that …
penso que,	(two more ways of saying "I think
acho que	that," etc., not found in this text)
a que eu vi tinha pintinhas	the one I saw had polka dots
cor (f.)	color
não tenho a certeza	I'm not sure
em todo o caso	anyway, in any case
Benfica	Portuguese soccer team
veio	he/she/it came (preterite of **vir**)
menos	except, aside from
nos venceram	they defeated us
o que tem a ver isso com …	what does that have to do with …
xadrez (m.)	checkered cloth (also: chess)
gaita (f.) de foles	bagpipes
de qualquer modo	anyway
haja …	may there be … (subjunctive of **haver**)
que lhe agrade	that pleases you (polite)

7

vejo	I see (present of **ver**)
esquisito	fussy
malcriado	rude
entredentes	(muttering) between one's teeth
em voz alta	aloud
ficava-lhe bem	it should suit you (polite)
bandeira (f.)	flag
ao pescoço (m.)	(hanging) from the neck
mas, afinal	but, after all
agora que a chuva já passou	now that the rain has stopped (lit. "passed")
vou-me embora	I'm going
para a próxima	next time
escolher	to choose
não são nada bons/boas	they (m./f.) aren't good at all

PRACTICE EXERCISE

Now answer these questions based on the preceding dialogue:

1 Por que razão se chama "chato" a este homem?

2 Descreva as gravatas todas que ele viu.

3 Que cor disse ele que era a sua favorita? E porquê?

4 Porque não quis ele (didn't want) a gravata italiana?

5 Qual foi a razão para ele não querer a gravata de xadrez?

6 Repita a expressão que este cliente usou como patriota.

7 Que lhe disse a empregada já desesperada?

8 E a resposta (reply) dele?

9 O que lhe chamou ela entredentes?

10 Do que lhe fez lembrar (what reminded him of) as cores encarnada e verde?

11 Por último, qual era a razão dele para estar naquela loja?

12 Que conselho (advice) lhe deu a empregada?

Week 8

- *past participles (the -ed form: "talked," etc.)*
- *the present perfect and past perfect*
- *reflexive verbs*
- *the reciprocal form ("each other," "one another")*
- *how to form the passive voice*
- *impersonal verbs ("it's raining")*

8.1 PAST PARTICIPLES (THE -ED FORM)

The past participle is formed by replacing the infinitive endings **-ar**, **-er**, or **-ir** with **-ado**, **-ido**, or **-ido**, respectively. Three regular examples are below:

infinitive		past participle	
dar	to give	**d<u>ado</u>**	given
vender	to sell	**vend<u>ido</u>**	sold
mentir	to lie	**ment<u>ido</u>**	lied

A number of common verbs have irregular past participles:

infinitive		past participle	
pôr	to put	**posto**	put
abrir	to open	**aberto**	opened
fazer	to do, to make	**feito**	done, made
escrever	to write	**escrito**	written
dizer	to say, to tell	**dito**	said, told
vir	to come	**vindo**	come
ver	to see	**visto**	seen
gastar	to spend	**gasto**	spent
ganhar	to earn, to win, to gain	**ganho**	earned, won, gained

Some verbs have two past participles: a regular form that remains invariable and is used with the auxiliary verb **ter** to form compound tenses and an irregular form that is used as an adjective with the auxiliary verbs **ser** and **estar**. When used as an adjective, the participle must agree with the noun it qualifies in number and gender.

8

The most frequent "double past participle" forms are:

infinitive	regular	irregular
aceitar to accept	**aceitado**	**aceito, aceite**
acender to light	**acendido**	**aceso**
enxugar to dry	**enxugado**	**enxuto**
expulsar to expel	**expulsado**	**expulso**
juntar to join	**juntado**	**junto**
limpar to clean	**limpado**	**limpo**
matar to kill	**matado**	**morto**
morrer to die	**morrido**	**morto**
pagar to pay	**pagado**	**pago**
prender to arrest	**prendido**	**preso**
romper to tear	**rompido**	**roto**
suspender to suspend	**suspendido**	**suspenso**

A roupa está quase enxuta.
The clothes are nearly dry.
Eu já tinha enxugado a louça.
I had already dried the dishes.
A luz está acesa. The light is on.
Ele já tinha acendido o fogão.
He had already lit the fire.

8.2 THE PRESENT AND PAST PERFECT

These compound tenses are formed, as in English, with the auxiliary verb **ter** ("to have") and the past participle of the main verb. In the present perfect, **ter** is conjugated in the present tense. In Portuguese, it is only used when the action is still happening—never when the action has been completely finished—so it often translates to the English present perfect continuous:

Tenho falado. I have been speaking.

The preterite is used in Portuguese to express an action completed in the past: **falei** ("I spoke") or ("I have spoken") (I have spoken in the past but am no longer speaking).

In the past perfect, **ter** is conjugated in the imperfect. It indicates an action in the past that occurred prior to another past action, the same as in English:

Tinha falado. I had spoken.

Here are a few examples showing how the different past tenses are used:

Ontem falei com a tua irmã.
Yesterday I spoke to your sister. (preterite)
Falava com a tua mãe.
I was speaking to your mother. (imperfect)
Ultimamente tenho falado muito francês.
Lately, I have been speaking a lot of French.
(present perfect)
Já tinha falado com o meu patrão antes de (você) me pedir para o fazer.
I had already spoken to my boss before you asked me to do it. (past perfect)

There is another past tense called the **pretérito mais-que-perfeito** (pluperfect), but it is rare in spoken Portuguese. We show how to form this simple (single word) tense in the Appendix (see p.222).

8

8.3 REFLEXIVE VERBS (E.G., **LEVANTAR-SE**)

A reflexive verb is used for actions that one does to oneself: that is, when the object of the verb is the same person or thing as the subject.

Reflexive verbs exist in English (e.g., "I wash myself," "I hurt myself") but are much more common in Portuguese. They are always used with a reflexive pronoun (e.g., **me**, **te**, **se**, etc.)—this is essential to include with the verb.

The pronoun comes before or after the verb according to the rules explained in section 6.5. Although the reflexive pronoun can be translated as "myself," "yourself," etc., in most cases it isn't natural in English to translate it at all.

Here are some common reflexive verbs:

levantar-se	to get up
lembrar-se de	to remember
esquecer-se de	to forget
sentar-se	to sit down
lavar-se	to wash oneself, to have a wash
barbear-se	to shave oneself
deitar-se	to go to bed, to lie down
vestir-se	to get dressed
despir-se	to get undressed
pentear-se	to comb one's hair
banhar-se	to bathe, to take a dip
divertir-se	to enjoy oneself
habituar-se a	to get used to
sentir-se	to feel
decidir-se a	to decide to

Não me lembrava da tua morada.
I couldn't remember your address.
Eles vão lavar-se.
They are going to wash (themselves).
Divertimo-nos muito na tua festa.
We enjoyed ourselves very much at your party.
Por favor, sente-se.
Please sit down.
Avie-se. *or* **Despache-se.**
Hurry up.
(Você) enganou-se.
You made a mistake.
Sirva-se.
Help yourself.

In English, "myself," "yourself," etc., are often used for emphasis ("I did it myself"). In Portuguese, this is expressed not with the reflexive pronoun but by the use of the adjective **mesmo** or **próprio**, which must agree with the subject in number and gender:

Eu própria lhe contei a história.
I (f.) myself told him the story.

Nós mesmos não queríamos ir.
We (ourselves) did not want to go.
Ele próprio veio falar comigo.
He came to speak to me himself.

8.4 RECIPROCAL FORMS ("EACH OTHER," "ONE ANOTHER")

The reflexive pronouns are also used to express reciprocal actions, conveying "each other" or "one another."

Nós encontrámo-nos por acaso.
We met each other by chance.
Eles amam-se. They love each other.
Elas não se conhecem. They don't know each other.
Nunca nos vimos. We have never seen each other.

To avoid ambiguity if a reciprocal meaning is intended, the phrase **um ao outro** ("one another") is sometimes added. This is especially the case with a reflexive verb. The phrase **um ao outro** needs to agree with the number and gender of the subjects involved:

um ao outro (two m. sing. subjects)
uma à outra (two f. sing. subjects)
uns aos outros (more than two m. or mixed
  m. & f. subjects)
umas às outras (more than two f. subjects)

Here's an example to illustrate this: **eles enganam-se** would normally mean "they are making a mistake." But it could mean "they are deceiving each other." To make the latter meaning absolutely clear, it is necessary to add the appropriate form of **um ao outro**:

A minha irmã e o cunhado enganam-se um ao outro.
My sister and brother-in-law deceive each other.

The passive is formed with the verb **ser** and the past participle, which must agree in number and gender with the subject. The passive is followed by the preposition **por** ("by"), combined with the articles in the usual way:

A carta foi escrita pela irmã.
The letter was written by his/her sister.
Ela é amada por todos.
She is loved by everyone.

The passive is not used as often in Portuguese as in English. It is more common in Portuguese to use the active voice with the pronoun **se**—this is similar to saying "one speaks" or "they speak," for example.

Aqui fala-se português.
Portuguese is spoken here.
Diz-se que ela é muito rica.
It is said that she is very rich.
Vê-se muita gente nas ruas no Natal.
Many people are seen in the streets at Christmas.
Aqui vendem-se jornais.
Newspapers are sold here.

This use of the active instead of the passive is especially apparent with **dizer**:

Disseram-me que ...
I was told that ... ("They told me that ...")
Dizem que ela é muito rica.
It is said that she is very rich. ("They say that ...")

Exercise 1

Translate the following:

1 Ela já tinha estudado português quando era criança.

2 Este ano tem havido muitos desastres de avião.

3 A mulher já estava morta quando o médico chegou.

4 As mesas já estavam postas, mas os convidados ainda não tinham chegado.

5 Eu nunca tinha visto tanta gente na minha vida.

6 Ela foi expulsa da escola.

7 Diz-se que a firma Agiota & Co. vai falir.

8 Não se deve enganar os outros.

9 Elas ainda não se tinham lavado.

10 Tem feito muito mau tempo.

VOCABULARY 1

criança (f.)	child (used for both genders)
desastre (m.)	accident, disaster
convidado/a	guest
tanta gente (f.)	so many people
vida (f.)	life
falir	to fold, to go bankrupt
enganar	to cheat
fazer bom/mau tempo	to be good/bad weather

8

8.6 IMPERSONAL VERBS (E.G., "IT'S RAINING")

There are a number of verbs that are used only in the third-person singular. The most common of these are **há** ("there is," "there are") and expressions describing the weather (such as **chove** "it's raining," **neva** "it's snowing"). Other examples are:

faz calor ("it's hot"), **faz frio** ("it's cold"), **faz sol** ("it's sunny"), **faz vento** ("it's windy").

Exercise 2

Translate the following:

1 Eles sentiam-se desanimados.
2 Levantei-me muito cedo.
3 Ele nunca se lembra dos meus anos.
4 Ela vestiu-se à pressa.
5 Ele cheira mal porque nunca se lava.
6 Como se diz "table" em português?
7 Eles olharam-se um ao outro.
8 Sirva-se enquanto a comida está quente.
9 Não nos conhecemos.
10 Eu queixei-me à polícia.
11 Vá-se embora.
12 Faz sol.
13 Esqueci-me dele.
14 Aqui vendem-se jornais ingleses.

VOCABULARY 2

desanimado	disappointed
cedo	early
meus anos	my birthday (or **o meu aniversário**)
pressa (f.)	hurry
cheirar	to smell
cheirar mal	to smell bad
olhar	to look at
comida (f.)	food
queixar-se	to complain
ir-se embora	to go away, to leave

8

Exercise 3

Translate the following:

1 I remember him.
2 I was not feeling well.
3 We complained about the food.
4 It has been raining a lot this year.
5 I had already mailed the letter.
6 A lot of wine is drunk in Portugal, but the Portuguese do not often get drunk.
7 The window was open.
8 The lottery was won by a poor woman.
9 My skirt was torn.
10 They were all arrested.
11 They looked at each other.
12 I have not been traveling this year.
13 One hears a lot of English music in Portugal.
14 I don't want to serve myself.
15 We saw each other by chance.
16 Newspapers are sold here.

VOCABULARY 3

pôr a carta no correio	to mail a letter
embriagar-se	to get drunk
com frequência	often, frequently
lotaria (f.)	lottery
saia (f.)	skirt
viajar	to travel
rasgar	to tear
ganhar	to win
prender, preso	to arrest, arrested

No restaurante / At the restaurant

SR. CARVALHO **Boa noite, tem uma mesa livre?**

EMPREGADO **O senhor não reservou?**

SR. CARVALHO **Não, não tive tempo, foi uma coisa decidida à última hora.**

EMPREGADO **Vou ver. Quantas pessoas são?**

SR. CARVALHO **Quatro. Preferia uma mesa ao pé da janela, pois está muito calor.**

EMPREGADO **Lamento muito, mas as mesas ao pé das janelas estão todas reservadas. Esta aqui agrada-lhe?**

SR. CARVALHO **Que remédio! Traga-nos a ementa, por favor, e a lista dos vinhos. O que nos recomenda?**

EMPREGADO **Recomendo-lhes o prato do dia que é especialidade cá da casa bacalhau de cebolada, ou então porco com ameijoas à alentejana que é um grande petisco português.**

SR. CARVALHO **Pois bem, traga esse para mim, bacalhau de cebolada para a minha filha, um bife à transmontana para a minha mulher e para o meu amigo frango na púcara.**

EMPREGADO **Que legumes?**

SR. CARVALHO **Ervilhas e batatas fritas para dois, puré de batata e feijão verde para outro e arroz e salada de alface e pepino para mim.**

EMPREGADO **E para beber, o que desejam?**

SR. CARVALHO **Vinho da casa. Uma garrafa de tinto e uma de branco. Traga também dois cafezinhos—um simples e um com leite para terminar o jantar, pois não queremos sobremesa. Queria também que me trouxesse a conta porque estamos com muita pressa; vamos a um concerto e não podemos chegar atrasados.**

8

No hotel / At the hotel

SR. JONES   Boa tarde. Chamo-me Jones.
Escrevi a marcar um quarto de casal
e um quarto individual.

RECECIONISTA   Um momento, se faz favor. Ora aqui
está. Senhor Jones, dois quartos para o
dia dezoito. Há aqui um problema:
aparentemente o meu colega deu estes
quartos a outras pessoas porque
pensava que os senhores não viessem.
Nós só reservamos os quartos até ao
meio-dia. É a época dos turistas e há
falta de acomodação.

SR. JONES   Que falta de consideração! Não sabe
que hoje em dia os aviões chegam e
partem quando lhes apetece? Não é
nossa culpa se chegamos atrasados. Nós
já lhe tínhamos escrito a fazer esta
marcação e os senhores responderam a
confirmá-la. Estamos cansados e
aborrecidos e agora não temos quartos.

RECECIONISTA   Peço imensa desculpa por este lapso da
nossa parte. Vou ver o que se pode
arranjar. [A rececionista regressa.]
Estamos com sorte. Falei com o gerente
que me disse para lhes dar um
apartamento de luxo que está
normalmente reservado. Os senhores
podem tê-lo pelo mesmo preço que os
quartos que tinham reservado. É claro
que só o podemos dar por duas noites.

SR. JONES   Não faz mal. A que horas servem o
pequeno-almoço?

RECECIONISTA   Das sete às nove e meia. Desejam
meia-pensão ou pensão completa?

SR. JONES   Preferimos pensão completa. E
gostaríamos que nos acordassem às
oito em ponto.

RECECIONISTA   Muito bem. Aqui está a vossa chave.

8

VOCABULARY 4

At the restaurant

Foi uma coisa decidida à última hora.	It was something decided at the last minute.
ao pé da	near, close to
Esta aqui agrada-lhe?	Will this one do?
bacalhau (m.) de cebolada (f.)	cod with onions (**bacalhau**, salted cod, is the national dish)
bife (m.) à transmontana	beef cooked in the style of Trás-os-Montes, a northern province of Portugal
porco (f.) com ameijoas (f.) à alentejana	pork with clams in the style of Alentejo, a province south of the River Tagus
frango (f.) na púcara	traditional Portuguese dish ("chicken in the pot"), which is cooked in an earthenware pot with herbs
legume (m.)	vegetable
ervilha (f.)	pea
batatas (f.) fritas	fried potatoes
puré (m.) de batata	mashed potato
feijão-verde (m.)	green bean
arroz (m.)	rice
alface (f.)	lettuce
pepino (m.)	cucumber
garrafa (f.)	bottle, carafe
vinho (m.) tinto/ branco	red/white wine
cafezinho* (m.)	coffee (diminutive form)
um café (m.) simples	black coffee (also known as **uma bica**)

* See footnote on page 135.

café (m.) com leite	white coffee (slang: **garoto**)
pois	as, for, because
sobremesa (f.)	dessert
conta (f.)	bill

At the hotel

marcar	to book
quarto (m.) de casal	double room
individual (m.&f.)	single room
falta de	shortage of
Que falta de consideração!	What a lack of consideration!
quando lhes apetece	when they feel like it
hoje em dia	nowadays
Não é nossa culpa.	It's not our fault.
marcação (f.)	booking
peço imensa desculpa	I'm so very sorry
lapso (m.) da nossa parte	oversight on our part
o que se pode arranjar	what can be done
gerente	manager (m. & f.)
Não faz mal.	It doesn't matter.
pequeno-almoço (m.) (in Brazil: **café da manhã**)	breakfast
meia-pensão (f.)	half board
pensão completa (f.)	full board
acordar	to wake someone up
chave (f.)	key

8

Practice

DIALOGUE

Uma senhora, que tinha visto um ladrão fugir de uma loja, foi à esquadra dar pormenores.

POLÍCIA O nome da senhora, faz favor, morada, lugar onde nasceu e data do seu nascimento.

SR.ª ANTUNES Chamo-me Maria Antunes, moro na Rua das Flores, n.º 18, 1.º Esq. e nasci em Viana do Castelo a 18 de outubro de 1970.

POLÍCIA ... nome de pai e mãe.

SR.ª ANTUNES Ó Senhor guarda, mas isso é necessário?

POLÍCIA É, senão não tinha perguntado.

SR.ª ANTUNES Bem, a minha mãe era Antónia Maria Antunes, a "padeira."

POLÍCIA Não estamos interessados em alcunhas. E o seu pai?

SR.ª ANTUNES Sei lá! Foi antes do meu tempo!

POLÍCIA Ora bem! Pode descrever-me o ladrão que viu?

SR.ª ANTUNES Vi-o muito bem. Era alto. Não. Estou enganada. Era mais baixo que alto. Moreno. Pensando bem, eu não podia ver-lhe a cara porque ele tinha um lenço por sobre o rosto.

POLÍCIA [em voz baixa] Estes pormenores vão ajudar-me muito, não há dúvida nenhuma. [em voz alta] Gordo ou magro?

SR.ª ANTUNES Gordo. Mais gordo do que eu.

POLÍCIA Cor do cabelo?

SR.ª ANTUNES Sei lá! Talvez loiro ... Estava muito escuro.

POLÍCIA Estava escuro? Como é possível quando o roubo aconteceu pela manhã?

SR.ª ANTUNES Ah, Senhor guarda, então foi outro roubo que eu vi.

POLÍCIA Na mesma loja? Um de manhã e outro de tarde?

SR.ª ANTUNES Pois, é verdade. Agora há tantos roubos!

POLÍCIA Desculpe-me, minha senhora, mas eu tenho de entrevistar outras pessoas. Obrigado por ter vindo. Adeus!

VOCABULARY

ladrão/ladra	thief
fugir	to run away, to flee
esquadra (f.)	police station
pormenor (m.)	detail
nasceu	he/she was born, you (polite) were born (preterite of **nascer**, to be born)
nascimento (m.)	birth
1.º Esq.	1st floor on the left
Senhor/Senhora guarda	(the polite way to address a police officer)
senão	otherwise
padeiro/a	baker
alcunha (f.)	nickname
Sei lá!	How should I know? God knows!
Ora bem!	Well now!
moreno	dark complexion (olive skin)
pensando bem	on second thought
cara (f.), rosto (m.)	face
lenço (m.)	handkerchief
não há dúvida nenhuma	there is no doubt at all
cabelo (m.)	hair
roubo (m.)	theft
aconteceu	it happened (preterite of **acontecer**, to happen)
Pois, é verdade!	So it is!, That's true!, Indeed!
entrevistar	to interview

8

PRACTICE EXERCISE

Now answer the following questions based on the previous dialogue:

1 Porque foi a senhora à Polícia?
2 Como se chamava ela? Onde tinha ela nascido e quando?
3 Qual era a morada dela?
4 Que alcunha tinha a mãe dela?
5 Qual foi a resposta dela quando o polícia lhe perguntou o nome do pai?
6 A senhora Antunes deu pormenores corretos a respeito do ladrão? (Dê exemplos.)
7 Porque não pôde ela ver o rosto do ladrão?
8 Quando tinha acontecido o roubo?
9 Na sua opinião, acha que a Sr.ª Antunes tinha visto algum roubo?
10 Que conclusão tirou deste caso?

Week 9

- *the subjunctive: uses and formation in the present, past, and future*
- *regular, irregular, and exceptional subjunctive forms*
- *"if" clauses*

9.1 THE PRESENT SUBJUNCTIVE

The next section will explain when the subjunctive is used, but first, let's look at its conjugations when referring to the present. To form the present subjunctive, in **-ar** verbs, the conjugation endings begin with **e**, whereas in **-er** and **-ir** verbs, the endings begin with **a**. The following table shows the regular conjugations for the present subjunctive for the three types of verb.

REGULAR VERBS

	falar	**comer**	**partir**
	to speak	to eat	to leave
eu	**fale**	**coma**	**parta**
tu	**fales**	**comas**	**partas**
ele, ela, você	**fale**	**coma**	**parta**
nós	**falemos**	**comamos**	**partamos**
eles, elas, vocês	**falem**	**comam**	**partam**

9

EXCEPTIONS AND IRREGULAR VERBS

The present subjunctive of irregular verbs is formed from the stem of the first-person singular of the present indicative (the present tense) and replacing the final **-o** with the endings **-a**, **-as**, **-a**, **-amos**, **-am**. For example:

fazer→ faço→ faça, faças, faça, façamos, façam

There are seven exceptions to this general rule.

ser	estar	dar
seja	esteja	dê
sejas	estejas	dês
seja	esteja	dê
sejamos	estejamos	dêmos
sejam	estejam	deem

saber	querer	ir
saiba	queira	vá
saibas	queiras	vás
saiba	queira	vá
saibamos	queiramos	vamos
saibam	queiram	vão

The seventh exception is **haver**, whose third-person singular present subjunctive is **haja**. (See also the table of verbs in the Appendix, p.213.)

9.2 USES OF THE SUBJUNCTIVE

Generally, the subjunctive expresses a possibility, doubt, wish, or something contrary to actual fact. It often corresponds to "may," "should," or "might" in English.

The subjunctive is used in subordinate clauses:

1 After a verb that expresses doubt, command, denial, wish, prohibition, permission, hope, request, regret, or following verbs of emotion ("to be sorry," "to be sad," "to be happy," "to fear"), etc.

main clause	subordinate clause
Quero	**que (você) saia.**
I want	you to leave. (literally, "that you leave")

Duvido que ele venha hoje.
I doubt whether he will come today.
(literally, "that he come")

Espero que ela esteja melhor.
I hope she is better.
Lamento que não possamos ir.
I regret that we are not able to come.
Folgo muito que seja assim.
I am so happy that it is so.
Temo que haja uma guerra.
I fear there may be a war.
Temos pena que eles não falem português.
We are sorry that they don't speak Portuguese.

2 In impersonal sentences.

É preciso que (vocês) estudem muito.
It is necessary for you to study hard.
(You must study hard.)
É provável que eu vá ao Japão.
I will probably go to Japan.

3 After verbs in the negative that express an opinion or thought.

Não acho que ele seja malcriado.
I don't think he is ill-mannered.
Não creio que o governo vá mudar.
I don't believe the government is going to change.

But note that the affirmative does not require the subjunctive:

Creio que o governo vai mudar.
I believe the government is going to change.

4 When speaking about something that may or may not exist.

Há aqui alguém que fale inglês?
Is there anyone here who speaks English?
Procuro uma casa que seja barata.
I am looking for a house that is cheap.

9

But compare these two statements:
Procuro uma casa que seja barata.
I am looking for a house that is cheap.
Procuro a casa que está anunciada no site.
I am looking for the house advertised on the website.

In the second example, the subject is specifically identified, so the subjunctive is not used.

5 After **talvez**, **tomara**, and **oxalá** (see week 5, conversation vocabulary).

Talvez seja verdade.
Maybe it is true.
Oxalá amanhã não chova.
I hope it doesn't rain tomorrow.
Tomara que ele não venha.
I hope he doesn't come.

Note that **tomara** is used in northern Portugal and Brazil, while **oxalá** (due to its Arabic derivation) is more frequently heard in Lisbon and southern Portugal.

6 After the following conjunctions (adverbial clauses).

a não ser que	unless
antes que	before
até que	until
ainda que	although, though
embora	though, although
mesmo que	even if
se bem que	though, although
contanto que	provided that
para que	so that, in order that
sem que	without

Janto consigo contanto que você pague a conta.
I'll dine with you provided you pay the bill.
Vamos agora sair antes que chova.
We're going to leave now before it rains.

Exercise 1

Translate the following (use **você** for "you"):

1 É preciso que eles estudem muito.

2 Oxalá eles não venham tarde.

3 Talvez eu saia amanhã.

4 Quero que (você) faça isso imediatamente.

5 Diga-lhe que não entre até que eu o chame.

6 Espero que a sua mulher esteja melhor.

7 Não acho que ele seja um bom jogador de futebol.

8 Queremos um homem que tenha a coragem das suas convicções.

9 Quer queira quer não queira, tenho de assistir à reunião amanhã.

10 Tell him not to go to the meeting.

11 Although I don't speak Portuguese very well, I understand everything.

12 Do you want me to bring you the wine list?

13 It is better for me to go now.

14 I don't think there are any newspapers today.

15 They are sorry you can't come tonight.

16 Please don't make any noise.

NOTE: remember that the polite form of the imperative uses the subjunctive.

9

VOCABULARY 1

até	until
jogador/a	player
quer queira quer não queira	whether I like it or not
reunião (f.)	meeting
lista (f.) dos vinhos	wine list
barulho (m.)	noise, commotion

The same rules apply to the imperfect subjunctive, but it is used to refer to the past. It is formed by removing the final **-r** from the infinitive and adding the endings below:

	falar to speak	**comer** to eat	**partir** to leave
eu	falasse	comesse	partisse
tu	falasses	comesses	partisses
ele, ela, você	falasse	comesse	partisse
nós	falássemos	comêssemos	partíssemos
eles, elas, vocês	falassem	comessem	partissem

The imperfect subjunctive of irregular verbs is formed by removing the ending **-mos** from the first-person plural of the preterite tense (see section 5.3) and adding the endings shown in the table above. For example:

fazer→ fize|mos (preterite)→ **fizesse, fizesses, fizessemos, fizessem**

There are no exceptions to this rule. Here is the imperfect subjunctive of some common irregular verbs:

dar   → de|mos→ **desse, desses, déssemos, dessem**
haver → houve|mos→ **houvesse, houvesses, houvéssemos, houvessem**
ser/ir → fo|mos→ **fosse, fosses, fôssemos, fossem**
ter   → tive|mos→ **tivesse, tivesses, tivéssemos, tivessem**
vir   → vie|mos→ **viesse, viesses, viéssemos, viessem**
ver   → vi|mos→ **visse, visses, víssemos, vissem**
estar → estive|mos→ **estivesse, estivesses, estivéssemos, estivessem**
dizer → disse|mos→ **dissesse, dissesses, disséssemos, dissessem**

9

The imperfect subjunctive is used in precisely the same circumstances as the present subjunctive, but when the verb in the main clause is in the past tense or conditional. For example:

Queria que ele arranjasse um emprego melhor.
I wanted him to get a better job.
Disse-lhe que não se fosse embora.
I told him not to go away.
Ele pediu-me que lhe dissesse que não podia vir.
He asked me to tell you that he couldn't come.

9.4 THE FUTURE SUBJUNCTIVE

The regular conjugations of the future subjunctive are as follows for the three verb types:

	falar to speak	**comer** to eat	**partir** to leave
eu	**falar**	**comer**	**partir**
tu	**falares**	**comeres**	**partires**
ele, ela, você	**falar**	**comer**	**partir**
nós	**falarmos**	**comermos**	**partirmos**
eles, elas, vocês	**falarem**	**comerem**	**partirem**

The future subjunctive of irregular verbs is formed by removing the ending **-mos** from the first-person plural of the preterite tense and adding the endings shown in the table above.

For example:
fazer → fize|mos→ **fizer, fizeres, fizermos, fizerem**

The future subjunctive is not a factual future. It is used when referring to possible or probable actions and events in a vague or unknown future.

The future subjunctive is introduced by the following conjunctions and adverbs:

quando when, whenever
se if
enquanto while
assim que as soon as
logo que as soon as
como as
conforme according to
o que whatever
quem whoever
aquele, aquela que whoever
aqueles, aquelas que those who
onde wherever (also used with the present subjunctive)

Here is an example to better illustrate the use of the future subjunctive:

Quando formos a Portugal, escrever-te-emos.
When we go (future subjunctive) to Portugal [which we may or may not], we will write to you.

9.5 SET EXPRESSIONS USING THE PRESENT AND FUTURE SUBJUNCTIVE

There are a number of set phrases in Portuguese that follow the pattern of present + future subjunctive. The most common of these are listed below:

Aconteça o que acontecer... Whatever happens ...
Haja o que houver... Whatever there may be ...
Seja quem for... Whoever it may be .../Whoever you may be ... (formal)
Diga o que quiser... Say what you like ...
Seja onde for... Wherever it may be ...
Faça como quiser... Do as you please ...

Many other permutations are possible, following the same basic pattern.

9.6 THE PERFECT SUBJUNCTIVE

These compound tenses are formed either with the present subjunctive or imperfect subjunctive of the auxiliary verb **ter**, followed by the past participle. Here is the present and past perfect subjunctive of **falar**.

	present perfect subj.	past perfect subj.
eu	**tenha falado**	**tivesse falado**
tu	**tenhas falado**	**tivesses falado**
ele, ela, você	**tenha falado**	**tivesse falado**
nós	**tenhamos falado**	**tivéssemos falado**
eles, elas, vocês	**tenham falado**	**tivessem falado**

These perfect subjunctive tenses are used in the same situations described in section 9.2. The following examples illustrate this:

After verbs of emotion

Espero que tenha vindo.
I hope he has come.
Esperava que tivesse vindo.
I hoped he had come.

After impersonal expressions

É provável que ele tenha ido a Lisboa.
It is likely that he has gone to Lisbon.
Era provável que ele tivesse ido a Lisboa.
It was likely that he had gone to Lisbon.

After verbs expressing an opinion in the negative

Não creio que tenham chegado.
I don't think they have arrived.
Não pensei que tivessem chegado.
I didn't think they had arrived.

9

Speaking of something that may or may not exist

Há aqui alguém que tenha visto o meu irmão?
Is there anyone here who has seen my brother?
Havia lá alguém que tivesse visto o teu irmão?
Was there anyone there who had seen your brother?

After **talvez**, **tomara**, and **oxalá**

Talvez tenham chegado.
Perhaps they have arrived.
Talvez não o tivessem ouvido.
Maybe they had not heard him.
Oxalá não tenha falado com os meus pais!
Hopefully he hasn't spoken to my parents!
Oxalá me tivesses dado ouvidos!
If only you had listened to me!
Tomara que ele não tivesse vindo.
I wish he had not come.

In adverbial clauses

Dar-lhe-ei as mercadorias contanto que tenha pagado a conta.
I'll give you the goods provided you've paid the bill.
Ter-lhe-ia dado as mercadorias contanto que (você) tivesse pagado a conta.
I would have given you the goods provided you had paid the bill.

The past perfect subjunctive is also used in "if" clauses referring to hypothetical or impossible situations. This is explained in more detail in the next section.

The word for "if" in Portuguese is **se**. The sequence of tenses used with **se** is determined according to the following system:

1 se referring to real facts

These sentences follow the pattern "If A is true, then B is true." In such cases, **se** must be followed by the indicative mood. For example:

Se ela compra uma propriedade, é porque tem dinheiro.
If she buys a property, it's because she has the money.
Se o marido chegava atrasado, ela inquietava-se.
If her husband arrived late, she used to worry.

In this type of sentence, it should normally be possible to substitute "when" for "if" without substantially changing the meaning. This is a useful identification test in "if" sentences.

2 se meaning "whether"

When **se** means "whether," it is always followed by the indicative mood, not the subjunctive. For example:

Não sei se ele vem.
I don't know whether he is coming.
Ao rei não lhe importava se morriam os súbditos.
The king did not care whether his subjects were dying.
Não me disse se eles tinham chegado.
He didn't tell me whether they had arrived.

3 se referring to possible events that have not yet happened

In sentences involving actions or events that are possible but have not yet been completed or fulfilled at the time of speaking, the future subjunctive must be used.

For example:

Se te lembrares, traz-me pêssegos de Portugal.
If you remember, bring me some peaches from Portugal.
Se formos a Portugal, trar-te-emos pêssegos.
If we go to Portugal, we will bring you peaches.

4 se referring to impossible or hypothetical events

When **se** refers to actions or events that are imaginary or
speculative, such as those invented for the sake of
argument, then the imperfect subjunctive is used.
For example:

Se fosse rico, iria dar uma volta ao mundo.
If I were rich, I would travel around the world.
Se ela tivesse dinheiro, comprava uma propriedade.
If she had money, she would buy a property.

When referring to actions or events in the past that might
have happened but did not actually take place, the past
perfect subjunctive is used. For example:

Se tivéssemos sabido disso, não teríamos dito nada.
If we had known that, we would not have said anything.

9

Exercise 2

Translate the following:

1 Foi pena que ele não pudesse vir.

2 Eu queria que vocês aprendessem português tão depressa quanto possível.

3 Não vi nenhuma casa que me agradasse.

4 Talvez ele tivesse já partido.

5 Se não fosse tão caro comprávamos uma quinta no Algarve.

6 Não queríamos que vocês trouxessem presentes.

7 Não sei se chove.

8 Se chover levo um guarda-chuva.

9 Enquanto os operários não recomeçarem o trabalho.não podemos aumentar a produção.

10 Vem a nossa casa quando quiseres.

11 Assim que você arranjar um emprego em Moçambique, diga-me.

12 Faça o que puder.

13 Convidem quem desejarem.

14 Aquele que quiser vir comigo que venha.

VOCABULARY 2

tão depressa quanto possível	as soon as possible
agradar	to please
guarda-chuva (m.)	umbrella
enquanto ... não	until
operário/a	worker, factory worker
recomeçar	to start again
aumentar	to increase
vem	come (familiar singular imperative of **vir**)
faça	he/she may do (present subj.)
convidar	to invite
desejar	to wish
que venha	may he/she come (pres. subj.)

9

Exercise 3

Translate the following:

1 As soon as you (familiar) can, please call me.
2 If he were not so lazy, he would not have lost that job.
3 It was necessary for them to call the police.
4 I told them to go away.
5 Whatever you say, I don't believe she is dishonest.
6 When I retire, I will write many books.
7 You may do as you wish.
8 Whatever happens and in spite of the weather, I will always love England.
9 There was no one who spoke English.
10 While you (pl.) are in my house, you are my guests.
11 I was sorry they were not able to come.
12 If you have lost this opportunity, it is because you wanted to.
13 Although they protested many times, the situation remained the same.
14 Perhaps she has told the truth.

VOCABULARY 3

preguiçoso, mandrião/mandriona (f.)	lazy
ir-se embora	to go away
desonesto	dishonest
reformar-se, aposentar-se	to retire
apesar de	in spite of
convidado/a	guest
oportunidade (f.)	opportunity
protestar	to complain, to protest
muitas vezes (f.)	many times
continuou na mesma	it remained the same

CONVERSATION

Uma avaria de automóvel / A car breakdown

JOAQUINA Olá, como estás? Então, por cá?

ANTÓNIO Sim cheguei ontem, às quatro da tarde. Ainda tentei telefonar-te, mas o teu telefone estava impedido.

JOAQUINA Pois estava. Era o meu marido que estava a fazer um telefonema para a França. Foi, por sinal, uma chamada caríssima, porque ele esteve a falar com o sócio francês dele, quase uma hora. E tu que me contas? Vieste de barco?

ANTÓNIO Não, por acaso não. Vim de automóvel por França e Espanha.

JOAQUINA O quê? Vieste sozinho por aí fora?

ANTÓNIO Não, não. Vim com dois amigos. A viagem correu muito bem até chegarmos à vizinhança de Salamanca. De repente, o carro deu um solavanco, derrapou para o sentido contrário e parou, felizmente sem nenhum embate. A surpresa foi tão grande e tudo se passou tão rapidamente que nem nos apercebemos do perigo. O susto veio depois do sucedido, por assim dizer. Descobrimos que era um furo no pneu. Infelizmente, tinha-me esquecido de trazer as ferramentas.

JOAQUINA Mas que disparate que fizeste!

ANTÓNIO Bem sei, e jurei nunca mais fazê-lo. Enfim, lá veio um carro que parou. Calcula tu que o motorista era um médico! Fiquei consternado, pois talvez ele estivesse a caminho da casa de um doente. Ele foi muito amável e mudou-nos a roda. Ainda bem que não me tinha esquecido do pneu sobresselente!

JOAQUINA Também digo! Foi este o único azar que tiveram?

9

ANTÓNIO	Não. Assim que passámos a fronteira, o carro teve outra avaria.
JOAQUINA	Não me digas! Mas que pouca sorte!
ANTÓNIO	É verdade! Graças a Deus, encontrámos um bom mecânico que verificou a embraiagem, afinou os travões e carregou a bateria. Foi uma despesa com que não contávamos e a falta deste dinheiro faz-nos uma grande diferença.
JOAQUINA	Mas naturalmente! Faria a qualquer pessoa. Olha! Vê lá que já são cinco horas. Ai, meu Deus, como o tempo voa! Tenho de me encontrar com o meu marido às cinco e meia para depois irmos à *soirée* de uma peça que tem tido muito êxito. Telefona-me amanhã para marcarmos o dia que vens a minha casa para jantar. Um dia que estejas disponível. Adeus, até amanhã.

VOCABULARY 4

avaria (f.)	breakdown (applies to anything out of order, like the TV, etc.)
Então, por cá?	What? You're over here?
tentar	to try, to attempt
impedido, ocupado	engaged, busy (telephone)
por sinal	as it happens, as a matter of fact
sócio/a	partner
contar	to tell
por acaso	actually, as a matter of fact
sozinho/a	alone
por aí fora	all that way
correu muito bem	it went very well
vizinhança (f.)	neighborhood, outskirts of
de repente, de súbito	suddenly
solavanco (m.)	jolt
derrapar	to skid
contrário	opposite

9

embate (m.)	collision
(in Brazil: **descontrole**)	
embater	to collide with
perigo (m.)	danger
susto (m.)	fright, shock
sucedido (m.)	event
por assim dizer	so to speak
furo (m.)	puncture in the tire
no pneu (m.)	
infelizmente	unfortunately
ferramenta (f.)	tool
disparate (m.)	foolish mistake, silly thing, nonsense
bem sei	I know
jurei	I swore
fiquei	I was dismayed, aghast
consternado/a	
roda (f.)	wheel
ainda bem	just as well, so pleased, so relieved
pneu (m.)	spare tire
sobresselente	
Também digo!	I'll say so! I agree!
o único azar (m.)	the only piece of bad luck
fronteira (f.)	frontier
que pouca sorte	what bad luck
Graças a Deus	Thank God
embraiagem (f.)	clutch
afinar os travões	to adjust the brakes
(in Brazil: **acertar os freios**)	
carregar a bateria	to charge the battery
despesa (f.)	expense
com que não	which we did not expect,
contávamos	which we weren't counting on
Olha!	Oh look!
vê lá	just imagine (fam. imperative)
como o tempo voa	how time flies
soirée (f.)	evening show (from the French)
peça (f.)	play
êxito (m.)	success
disponível	available, free

9

Practice

ANA As férias estão quase a acabar. Quem me dera que elas nunca acabassem.

PEDRO Eu também seria mais feliz se não tivesse de trabalhar. Mas, no ano que vem vou ter este desejo, isto é, se eu obtiver a minha licenciatura.

ANA Que sorte! E o que vais fazer?

PEDRO Vou visitar Macau, assim como Hong Kong e, já que estou naquela parte do mundo, irei visitar o Japão e a China, se Deus quiser.

ANA E quem vai pagar isso tudo?

PEDRO O meu pai, claro. Ele tinha-me dito que se eu não "chumbasse" nos exames, ele me oferecia esta viagem. Oxalá ele não falte ao prometido.

ANA Claro que ele não vai fazer isso. Quem me dera que o meu fizesse o mesmo. Não seria bom se nós fôssemos juntos?

PEDRO Seria. Mas, mesmo que não vás comigo, eu lembrar-me-ei sempre de ti. E, aconteça o que acontecer, a nossa amizade não morrerá.

ANA Espero que não.

VOCABULARY

Quem me dera!	How I wish! (**pretérito mais-que-perfeito** of **dar**)
obtiver	if I get, obtain (future subj. of **obter**)
licenciatura (f.)	BA, university degree
se Deus quiser	God willing (future subj. of **querer**)
se eu não chumbasse	if I didn't flunk (the exams) (imperfect subj.)
faltar ao prometido	to go back on one's word, to fail in a promise
se fôssemos juntos	if we went together (imperfect subj. of **ir**)
amizade (f.)	friendship

PRACTICE EXERCISE

Answer the questions based on the dialogue:

1 O que desejam o Pedro e a Ana?
2 O Pedro que espera fazer no próximo ano?
3 Quem lhe oferece essa viagem?
4 Que condição lhe impôs o pai?
5 Por que razão ele vai visitar Macau e Hong Kong?
6 Que receia o Pedro?
7 Qual é o desejo da Ana?
8 Que lhe promete o Pedro?
9 Se o/a estudante tivesse muito dinheiro, o que faria?
10 Concorda que seria bom nunca trabalhar?

9

Week 10

10.1 THE PERSONAL INFINITIVE

The personal infinitive is unique to Portuguese. It is an infinitive with conjugation endings to indicate the person to whom the infinitive refers. It can serve to grammatically simplify sentences, for instance, by replacing the more complicated subjunctive.

The formation of the personal infinitive is the same for all verbs, without exception. It has only one set of endings, whether the verb is regular or irregular, and it can be used with subject pronouns ("I," "you," "he," "she," etc.).

Conjugating the personal infinitive

	singular	plural
1st person	**falar**	**falarmos**
2nd person (familiar)	**falares**	**falarem**
3rd person (& 2nd person polite)	**falar**	**falarem**

USES OF THE PERSONAL INFINITIVE
1 In place of the subjunctive.

The personal infinitive can replace the subjunctive after such verbs as **lamentar**, **agradar**, **surpreender**, **folgar**, **estranhar**, **recear**, and similar verbs.

subjunctive: **Surpreende-me que estejas cansado.**
pers. inf.: **Surpreende-me estares cansado.**
It surprises me that you are tired.
subjunctive: **Lamento que estejamos atrasados.**
pers. inf.: **Lamento estarmos atrasados.**
I am sorry (regret) that we are late.

NOTE: When expressing a wish or hope, use the subjunctive if the subject of the second verb is different from the subject in the main clause:

Espero que venhas amanhã.
I hope you come tomorrow.

The personal infinitive can also replace the subjunctive in impersonal expressions:

subjunctive: **E bom que estudes muito para que fiques aprovada no exame.**

pers. inf.: **E bom estudares muito para ficares aprovada no exame.**
It's good that you study hard so that you pass the exam.

subjunctive: **É pena que não estejam aqui.**

pers. inf.: **É pena não estarem aqui.**
It's a shame they are not here.

It can also replace the subjunctive after certain conjunctions, if they can be turned into prepositions, i.e., **para que = para**; **até que = até**; **sem que = sem**, etc. **antes que** becomes **antes de**; **depois que** becomes **depois de**:

subjunctive: **Partiram sem que lhes disséssemos adeus**.

pers. inf.: **Partiram sem lhes dizermos adeus.**
They left without us saying goodbye to them.

subjunctive: **Vou sair antes que chova.**

pers. inf.: **Vou sair antes de chover.**
I'm going out before it rains.

subjunctive: **Não te perdoo até que peças perdão.**

pers. inf.: **Não te perdoo até me pedires perdão.**
I'm not forgiving you until you apologize to me.

The following conjunctions must use the subjunctive: **embora, contanto que, ainda que, se bem que, a não ser que; mesmo que** (which turns into **mesmo se**) and **logo que** both require the future subjunctive.

10

2 To express "on doing something".

The personal infinitive is a simple and convenient way of expressing the English construction "on" + present participle. It can be used in combination with past, present, and future tenses. For example:

Ao chegarem, encontraram-se logo com o Primeiro-Ministro.
On arriving, they immediately met the Prime Minister.

In English, to avoid ambiguity, we would say, "On their arrival … ." But in Portuguese, the ending **-em** clearly identifies "them" as the subject. Another example:

Ao entrarmos, vimos o ladrão.
On entering (as we entered), we saw the thief.
(Note: Do not use subject pronouns after **ao** + pers. inf.)

3 After the preposition **a** in a concessional clause.

A portarem-se deste modo, vão/irão parar na prisão.
If they behave in this way, they will end up in prison.

4 To express the reason for doing something.

por plus the personal infinitive is a succinct way of replacing **porque** + indicative. For example:

indicative: **Não te escrevemos porque não sabíamos a tua morada.**
pers. inf.: **Não te escrevemos por não sabermos a tua morada.**
We did not write to you because we did not know your address.
indicative: **Inácio partiu porque chegou a sua sogra.**
pers. inf.: **Inácio partiu por chegar a sua sogra.**
Inácio departed because his mother-in-law arrived.

5 Colloquial use to express irony, sarcasm, or incredulity.

When the personal infinitive is used in this way, the meaning is conveyed as much by intonation as by the form of verb. Such expressions are usually best rendered as below:

Tu? Estudares?
You? Studying?
(*or* What? You're actually studying?)
Nós? Mentirmos por tua causa?
Us? Tell lies on your account?
(*or* Do you really expect us to tell lies for your sake?)

Exercise 1

Translate the following:

1 Este livro é para lermos.
2 Não quero comprar o carro sem tu concordares.
3 É pena não poderes vir no próximo domingo.
4 Foi bom trazerem os vossos casacos porque vai estar frio.
5 Receio estarem zangados comigo.
6 Não vieram por estarem cansados.
7 Foi impossível irmos à tourada.
8 Vocês? Ganharem a taça mundial?
9 They are going to leave before we arrive.
10 It was impossible for us to see the minister.
11 It surprises me, you (familiar sing.) saying a thing like that.
12 I said goodbye to them before they left.
13 I cannot give an opinion until we know everything.
14 We didn't have lunch because we didn't have time.

VOCABULARY 1

concordar	to agree
casaco (m.)	coat
recear	to fear
zangado	cross, angry
tourada (f.)	bullfight
taça (f.) mundial	World Cup (In Brazil: **copa do mundo**)
uma coisa assim/uma coisa destas	a thing like that

10.2 THE PRESENT PARTICIPLE (THE -ING FORM: E.G., "SAYING," "DOING," ETC.)

The present participle is formed by removing the **-r** from the infinitive ending and adding **-ndo** to the stem.

falar > falando	speaking
comer > comendo	eating
abrir > abrindo	opening

The use of the present participle in Portuguese is much more limited than in English. It cannot be used as a noun. It is used principally in adverbial clauses.

For example:
Lá continuaram a sua viagem, passando por aldeias, atravessando rios e subindo montanhas.
There they continued their journey, passing through villages, crossing rivers, and ascending mountains.

The Portuguese present participle can be used to translate "on" + present participle in English ("on doing") only when the action described by the present participle precedes the action of the verb in the main clause, or the two actions are simultaneous.

For example:
Dizendo isto, desapareceu.
On saying this, he disappeared.

Sendo assim, aceito com prazer.
This being the case, I accept with pleasure.

10.3 USES OF THE INFINITIVE

It is important to note that there are some instances in Portuguese in which the infinitive must be used, whereas in English, we use the present participle.

1 Continuous actions

In Portuguese, continuous actions are not expressed by the present participle, as they are in English. Instead, the infinitive is used with the appropriate form of **estar a**.

For example:
Estou a ler o jornal.
I am reading the paper.
Estavam a jogar futebol.
They were playing football.

However, when the action takes place over a prolonged period of time, it is preferable to use **andar a** + infinitive instead of **estar a**.

For example:
Ando a aprender português.
I am learning Portuguese.
Andam a construir uma nova câmara municipal.
They are building a new town hall.

As we've seen, it's also common in Portuguese to use the simple present and imperfect tenses to express continuous action in the present and past, respectively.

For example:
Aonde vais? Where are you going?
Que fazias? What were you doing?

10

In Brazilian Portuguese, however, the present participle is used in continuous tenses. Thus, it follows the English usage exactly:

Eles estão jogando futebol.
They are playing football.

2 In place of the gerund

In English, when the present participle is used as a noun, it is called a gerund (e.g., "I love dancing"). In Portuguese, the infinitive performs the function of a gerund.

For example:
É proibido fumar. No smoking allowed.

10.4 POR AND PARA

The prepositions **por** and **para** are easily confused by English speakers, as they can both be used to mean "for" in various situations as well as having other meanings in different contexts. The examples below will help distinguish between their uses, but it is important to carefully observe how they are employed when you come across them in speech or writing and try to memorize individual cases when this doesn't seem obvious.

USES OF POR
1 On behalf of, on account of

Eu pago a conta por você.
I will pay the bill for you. (on your behalf)
Ele lutou por ti.
He fought for you. (on your behalf or on your account)

2 In exchange for

Troco este casaco pelo seu chapéu.
I will give you this coat for your hat.

3 In expressions of time

por is used in a number of time expressions, mainly relating to duration or frequency. When it relates to frequency, it corresponds exactly to the use of "per" in English:

Eles vieram por duas semanas.
They came for two weeks. (duration)
Ele vai a Paris duas vezes por semana.
He goes to Paris twice a week. (frequency)
Pela primeira vez, vi que ela era bonita.
For the first time, I noticed that she was pretty.

4 **por** meaning "by," "through," "along," etc.

In most contexts, "by" is translated by **por**. It is also used to translate "through" and "along," especially with verbs of motion. It is frequently used in conjunction with other adverbs to imply motion. For example:

Vou pela praia.
I'm going along the beach.
Viajo para Portugal por França.
I travel to Portugal through France.
Vamos pela TAP, naturalmente.
We are going by TAP, of course.
É por aqui ou por ali?
Is it this way or that way?
Por onde desapareceu?
Where did it disappear to?

USES OF **PARA**
1 Destination, purpose

In this case, **para** is used mainly with verbs of motion and in expressions where giving or sending is implied:

Ele vai para o Brasil. He is going to Brazil.
(See section 10.5 for more on **para** meaning "to.")

10

Estas flores são para ti.
These flowers are for you.
Para que faz (você) isso?
What are you doing that for?

2 Expressions of fixed time

While **por** is used to express duration ("the time within which ...") or frequency, **para** refers to "time at which ...":

Tenho hora marcada para as três.
I have an appointment for three o'clock.

3 "About to"

Os pais dele estão para chegar.
His parents are about to arrive.
Estava para comprar um carro alemão, mas mudei de ideias.
I was about to buy a German car, but I changed my mind.

4 Viewpoint

Esse trabalho é muito difícil para mim.
This work is very difficult for me.
Este casaco é demasiado grande para ele.
This coat is too big for him.

10.5 THE PREPOSITIONS A AND PARA

As we saw in section 2.6, **a** can mean "at" and "to"; **para**, apart from its other meanings, can also mean "to." When referring to a destination, **para** expresses permanency or a longer duration than **a**. For example, when going to work in the morning or returning from it at the end of the day, you'd say:

Vou para o escritório. I'm going to the office.
Vou para casa. I'm going home.

But if you were dropping in for a fleeting visit, you'd say:

Vou ao escritório buscar a correspondência.
I'm going to the office to get my mail.
Vou a casa buscar as chaves.
I'm going to my house to get the keys.

Similarly:
Ela vai para o Brasil trabalhar.
She is going to Brazil to work.
Vamos a Paris passar o fim de semana.
We are going to Paris to spend the weekend.

10.6 SPECIAL USES OF THE DEFINITE ARTICLE

In previous sections, we've seen that in Portuguese, unlike in English, the definite article is usually required before possessive adjectives. However, note that in Brazil, the definite article is not necessary when speaking about family members. For example:

a minha irmã (Portugal)/**minha irmã** (Brazil) my sister

Generally, when the relationship between the possessor and the thing possessed is unmistakably clear—such as in the case of parts of the body or personal clothing—the possessive adjective is omitted altogether, and only the definite article is used. For example:

O meu pai abanou a cabeça.
My father shook his ("the") head.
O homem tirou o chapéu.
The man took off his ("the") hat.

The most common occasions when the definite article is used in Portuguese but not in English are:

Before names of people
a Rita, o José, a dona (D.ª) Amélia, o senhor doutor Silva, etc.

Before continents
a Europa, a África

Before countries
a Inglaterra

Before provinces
a Estremadura, o Alentejo
(Portugal and its former overseas colonies do not require the definite article, although the autonomous regions of the Azores and Madeira do: **os Açores, a Madeira**.)

Before cities
but these do not require the article unless they have a physical meaning, as in **o Porto, o Rio de Janeiro**.

Before rivers
o Tejo the Tagus, **o Tamisa** the Thames,
o Sena the Seine

The definite article is used before **Senhor**, **Senhora**, and **Menino/a** except in correspondence—in addressing an envelope, for example.

Before generalized nouns
When referring to a category of persons or things in general, the definite article is used. For example:

As cidades cada vez estão maiores.
Cities (in general) are getting bigger and bigger.
Os cães ladram.
Dogs (in general) bark.

In expressions of time, in combination with the prepositions **em** and **a**

na quarta-feira passada last Wednesday
no inverno in winter
às três horas at three o'clock

10

Exercise 2

Translate the following:

1 Não tenho tempo para escrever cartas.
2 A Sr.ª (senhora) D.ª (dona) Amélia vai ao médico na quarta-feira.
3 A minha irmã vai para o hospital na terça-feira para fazer uma operação à garganta.
4 Digo-lhe isto para seu bem.
5 Não foi por querer que o magoei.
6 No mês passado, fui a Paris visitar a minha tia.
7 Muito obrigada pela sua amabilidade.
8 Por mim não me importo.
9 I have no news for you. (familiar sing.)
10 He fought for the rights of humankind.
11 He has gone to London on business.
12 Are you (m. formal sing.) going home now?
13 António went to Africa to work.
14 I beg your pardon for arriving late.
15 I am going to bed.

VOCABULARY 2

garganta (f.)	throat
por querer/ de propósito	on purpose
magoar	to hurt
não me importo	I don't mind

10

CONVERSATIONS

Acidentes e incidentes / Accidents and incidents

1 Catástrofes domésticas

SENHORA A **Hoje tem sido um daqueles dias de azar. O meu autoclismo recusa-se a funcionar, o cano do lava-louças está entupido e a torneira da banheira continua a pingar sem cessar.**

SENHORA B **Você tem de chamar um canalizador.**

SENHORA A **Sim, e não é só ele. A campainha da porta não toca, não sei porquê. A televisão está avariada e os eletricistas estão em greve. A minha mulher a dias não está em greve, mas fez gazeta hoje, dizendo que tinha uma grande constipação. E amanhã tenho estes convidados que chegam de Londres para virem passar uma semana connosco. Valha-me Deus! Que vou fazer?**

SENHORA B **Coitada! Mas não se apoquente desse modo porque não remedeia nada. Eu aconselhava-a a que recebesse os seus convidados muito calmamente e que lhes apresentasse a situação de uma maneira cómica. Diga-lhes que o ambiente é primitivo. Os ingleses têm um extraordinário sentido de humor e apreciam muito as pessoas que fazem brincadeira de tudo quanto é aborrecido.**

10

2 Fogo

HOMEM A **Socorro! Socorro! Chamem os bombeiros e a ambulância.**

HOMEM B **O que é? Onde é o incêndio?**

HOMEM A **É ali no mato, está a alastrar-se rapidamente. E oiço crianças a chorar e pessoas a gritar. Devem ser famílias que foram lá hoje fazer piquenique. Com um dia tão lindo! E é por isso que as labaredas avançam rapidamente porque está tudo tão seco! Oxalá não haja mortos ou ferimentos graves.**

HOMEM B **Se Deus quiser não haverá. Olhe, cá estão as ambulâncias e os bombeiros. Levaram só dois minutos. São muito competentes!**

HOMEM A **Que pena o mato ficar queimado! Tinha árvores tão antigas e majestosas!**

HOMEM B **Possivelmente foi um irresponsável que atirou o cigarro para o chão, sem pensar nas consequências.**

3 Uma anedota

No comboio, um passageiro viu um outro cuspir no chão. Muito chocado com esta ação imprópria, ele decidiu dizer ao outro:

—O senhor não leu o aviso na parede que diz "É proibido aos senhores passageiros cuspirem no chão"?

—Sim, li. Mas eu não sou passageiro, sou empregado da Carris.

10

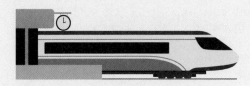

VOCABULARY 3

For Conversation 1

azar (m.)	bad luck
autoclismo (m.)	flush (of the cistern)
cano (m.)	pipe of the sink
do lava-louças (m.)	
entupido	blocked
torneira (f.)	tap, faucet
banheira (f.)	bathtub
pingar	to drip
canalizador/	plumber
(in Brazil: **bombeiro/a, tanoeiro/a**)	
campainha (f.)	doorbell
da porta (f.)	
tocar	to call (also, to play music)
A televisão (f.)	The TV is out of order.
está avariada.	
em greve	on strike
homem/mulher	cleaner, domestic help
a dias or **empregado/a doméstico/a**	
Fez gazeta hoje.	She has not turned up today.
uma grande	a nasty cold
constipação (f.)	
convidado/a	guest
Valha-me Deus.	May God help me.
Coitado/a!	Poor you!
Não se apoquente desse modo.	Don't worry yourself like that. Don't upset yourself in this way.
Não remedeia.	It doesn't help. It doesn't solve anything.
aconselhava	I would advise (imperfect of **aconselhar**, to advise)
ambiente (m.)	environment
sentido (m.) de humor (m.)	sense of humor
fazer brincadeira (f.) de	to make fun of (**brincadeira** joke, game)

10

For Conversation 2

Socorro!	Help!
bombeiros (m.)	firefighters
incêndio (m.)	fire
mato (m.)	woods, undergrowth, scrub
alastrar-se	to spread
oiço	I hear
chorar	to cry
gritar	to shout, to scream
labareda (f.)	flame
avançar	to advance
seco	dry
morto	dead (or dead person)
ferimento (m.) grave	serious injury
se Deus quiser	God willing
Olhe!	Look! (polite)
competente	competent, skilled
Que pena!	What a shame!
queimado	burned
atirar	to throw
cigarro (m.)	cigarette
chão (m.)	floor, ground

For Conversation 3

cuspir	to spit
aviso (m.)	notice
parede (f.)	wall
empregado/a da Carris	railway employee (Carris is the name of a Lisbon public transport company)

10

Practice

Fill in each blank with the appropriate form of the verb shown in brackets. When the subject pronoun is shown after the verb form, this indicates that the personal infinitive is required. You'll find the answers in the key on p.242.

Querida amiga Antónia,

Recebi a tua estimada carta há já um mês e … [sentir-se] muito envergonhada por não te ter … [escrever, *past part.*] ainda.

Acredita que não … [ser] falta de amizade ou indiferença, mas falta de tempo. Tudo … [parecer] ter … [conspirar, *past part.*] para que eu não … [ter] um minuto de vagar. Tenho … [ter] pessoas de família em minha casa, uma delas, doente. Ao mesmo tempo, as obras na minha casa … [começar]. E já não … [ser, *imp.*] sem tempo! Em face disto tudo, acho que tu … [ir] desculpar-me.

Como … [estar] vocês? Como … [estar] o tempo aí? Já … [eu, saber] que tem … [chover, *past part.*] muito no Algarve. Ainda bem! Oxalá chova mais, pois vocês … [sofrer] uma prolongada seca, no ano passado, a qual … [dever] ter … [causar, *past part.*] grande prejuízo à agricultura. Quando me … [lembrar] da boa fruta e legumes que eu … [comer] nessa paradisíaca região! Aqui tem … [chover, *past part.*] muito, … [eu, estar] farta de chuva. Se nós … [poder] exportar chuva para o vosso país, … [estar, *cond.*] mais ricos e vocês em melhor situação … [ficar, *cond.*].

… [Eu, agradecer]-te muito o teu convite para … [ir, nós] a Portugal para vossa casa. Vocês … [ser] muito amáveis, mas … [eu, crer] que não … [ir] ser possível porque já … [nós, aceitar] o convite que a tua irmã nos … [fazer] para … [passar, nós] o … verão em Lisboa e … [assistir, nós] ao Torneio Europeu de Futebol que tanto … [querer, nós] ver. Talvez tu … [poder] ir

10

também. Se vocês ... [ir], diz-me para ... [poder, nós] estar lá todos juntos. Espero que ... [haver] quartos para todos. Deste modo, eu ... [matar, i*mp.*] dois coelhos de uma cajadada. Mas ... [dizer] me com antecedência porque tenho que marcar as passagens muito antes, senão não ... [conseguir, *fut.*] ter nenhum lugar.

Bem, por hoje termino. Cá fico aguardando as tuas notícias que me ... [dar] sempre muito prazer, ... [prometer, *pres. part.*] ser pontual para próxima vez, envio beijinhos aos teus filhos, uma festinha ao cão, cujo nome não me ... [recordar], um abraço à tua mãe, cumprimentos ao teu marido e, para ti, muitas saudades desta tua amiga muito grata.

Mariana

VOCABULARY

envergonhado	ashamed, embarrassed
amizade (f.)	friendship
vagar	to loiter, to wander
obras (f.) (na casa)	building work (at home)
Já não era sem tempo!	About time too!
prolongada seca (f.)	long drought
prejuízo (m.)	loss, damage
legumes (m. pl.)	vegetables
paradisíaco	like paradise
farta de	fed up with
agradecer	to thank
juntos	together
matar dois coelhos (m.)	to kill two birds with
de uma cajadada (f.)	one stone
com antecedência	in advance, beforehand
marcar as passagens (f.)	to book the flights
senão	otherwise
cá fico aguardando	I'm looking forward to it
festinha (f.)	pat, caress
saudade (f.)	love ("yearning," "longing")

10

Week 11

- Reading practice
- Writing letters, both informal and formal

Reading practice

Uma viagem pela Europa

Quando recebi o convite para um casamento em Verona, na Itália, fiquei muito entusiasmada. Podia apanhar o comboio e viajar pela Europa! Assim, numa manhã de julho, parti com uma mochila às costas, um passe de comboio e uma carteira cheia de euros e comecei a minha aventura!

Apanhei um comboio de Londres para Amesterdão e passei um fim de semana agradável a andar de bicicleta pelos canais e a experimentar os deliciosos queijos holandeses. Depois, parti para Munique e explorei o seu enorme parque central, o Englischer Garten. De seguida, viajei pelos Alpes até Lyon e depois pela costa oeste de França. A viagem levou vários dias, mas a paisagem era tão espetacular que não me importei. Após uma paragem em Bordéus para desfrutar do seu famoso vinho, cruzei a fronteira com Espanha e viajei ao longo da costa norte, parando para experimentar os pintxos em San Sebastián e visitar a catedral de Santiago de Compostela. Em Portugal, explorei a encantadora Baixa de Lisboa de elétrico. Depois, regressei a Espanha onde visitei o Museu do Prado em Madrid e descobri a extraordinária arquitetura de Gaudí em Barcelona. Daí, voltei a França e passei alguns dias nas requintadas estâncias balneares da Côte d'Azur.

Quando cruzei a fronteira italiana e cheguei a Génova, sabia que a minha maravilhosa viagem estava quase a terminar. Mas havia ainda um sítio a visitar: a cidade histórica e romântica de Verona. O casamento foi incrível e desfrutei de uma das melhores refeições da minha vida. Foi o final perfeito de uma viagem inesquecível.

VOCABULARY

casamento	wedding	**agradável**	enjoyable
parti	set off	**canais**	canals
mochila às costas	backpack	**deliciosos**	delicious
		explorei	explored
passe de comboio	rail pass	**enorme**	huge
		paisagem	scenery

11

A tour of Europe

When I received an invitation to a wedding in Verona, Italy, I was really excited. I could take the train and go on a tour of Europe! So, one morning in July, I set off with a backpack, a rail pass, and a wallet full of euros and began my adventure!

I took a train from London to Amsterdam and spent an enjoyable weekend cycling along the canals and trying delicious Dutch cheeses. Then I went to Munich and explored its huge central park, the Englischer Garten. Next, I traveled through the Alps to Lyon and then to the west coast of France. It took several days, but the scenery was so spectacular that I didn't mind. After stopping in Bordeaux to enjoy its famous wine, I crossed the border into Spain and traveled along the north coast, stopping to try pinxos in San Sebastián and visit the cathedral in Santiago de Compostela. I explored Lisbon's charming old town by streetcar, visited the Prado museum in Madrid, and discovered the extraordinary architecture of Gaudí in Barcelona. From there, I returned to France and spent a few days in the stylish seaside resorts of the Côte d'Azur.

When I crossed the Italian border and arrived in Genoa, I knew my amazing tour was almost over. But I had one place left to visit: the historic and romantic city of Verona. The wedding was incredible and I had one of the best meals of my life. It was the perfect end to an unforgettable trip.

espetacular	spectacular	**arquitetura**	architecture
não me		**requintadas**	stylish
importei	didn't mind	**estâncias**	
encantadora	charming	**balneares**	seaside resorts
descobri	discovered	**incrível**	incredible
extraordinária	extraordinary	**inesquecível**	unforgettable

11

Writing letters

Here is some guidance on how to begin and end correspondence, followed by a sample business letter. Refer also to the personal letter in week 10's Practice section on p.190.

The date is generally prefaced by the name of the place the sender is writing from:
Londres, 23 de setembro de 2021 or **Londres, 09-23-2021**.

(Note that months are officially spelled with an initial lowercase rather than capital letter; however, many Portuguese speakers write the months with an initial capital letter, so you may see this written both ways.)

If writing to friends or colleagues, begin with **Querido** or **Querida...** (Dear ...), depending, of course, on the friend's gender. Equally, you could start with **Caro/a...**:

Querida Natália; Caro Paulo; Querida amiga

1 Depending on the degree of familiarity or friendship, use either the familiar **tu** or the polite **você**:

A
Então, como vais? Já viste o Pedro? Dá-lhe um abraço da minha parte. Quando vens a Londres? Já sinto saudades de ti e de Sintra.
Well, how are things with you? Have you seen Peter? Give him a hug from me. When are you coming to London? I'm missing you and Sintra.

B
Espero que (você) esteja bem e o seu marido vá melhor. Quando é que vocês vêm cá?
I hope you are well and that your husband is better. When are you (pl.) coming here?

2 There is another form of address that is neither familiar nor formal but is friendly and at the same time courteous. It uses the first name followed by the verb conjugations for **você** and third-person pronouns. This style is preferred by those who don't like using **você**:

Cara Rita, Como está? Há quanto tempo que ando para lhe escrever! Infelizmente não tenho tido um momento para o fazer. Eu sei que a Rita vai desculpar-me. Quero agradecer à Rita o seu amável convite para eu ir a Lisboa passar o Carnaval consigo …
Dear Rita, How are you? I have been meaning to write to you for so long! Unfortunately, I haven't had one moment to do so. I know that you will forgive me. I want to thank you for your kind invitation for me to come to Lisbon and spend Carnival with you …

3 In formal or business letters, "Dear sir" or "Dear madam" is expressed by **Ex.ᵐᵒ Senhor** or **Ex.ᵐᵃ Senhora**. The equivalent of "Dear sirs" is **Ex.ᵐᵒˢ Senhores** or simply **Senhores**.

Ex.ᵐᵒ/ᵃ is an abbreviation of **Excelentíssimo/a**. In Brazil, the abbreviation is written as **Ilmo./a.**, which is short for **Ilustríssimo/a**.

Thereafter in such letters, "you" is normally translated by **V. Ex.ᵃ** for **Vossa Excelência** (both genders, singular) and **V. Ex.ᵃˢ** in the plural. (In Brazil: **V.S.a (Vossa Senhoria)**, plural **V.S.as**) Thus:

Acuso a receção (or: o recebimento) de vossa carta datada 23-09-2021, na qual V. Ex.ᵃˢ nos perguntavam se ainda estávamos interessados em manter relações com a vossa firma…
I acknowledge receipt of your letter dated September 23, 2021, in which you were asking if we were still interested in maintaining our relationship with your firm …

4 When it comes to ending your letter, as you'd expect, the closing depends on how well you know your correspondent. The following examples refer to the contexts in paragraphs 1A, 1B, 2, and 3.

11

(1A)
Um grande abraço para ti; Um beijinho; Saudades
A big hug, Kisses, Missing you (all equivalent to "Love")

saudades, which means "longing," "yearning," can be used to signify anything from "love" to "regards."

(1B and 2)
Abraços para si e o seu marido
Love ("embraces") to you and your husband
Cumprimentos ao seu marido/à sua família
Best regards to your husband/to your family

Carta comercial em resposta a uma queixa

Lisboa, 8 de maio de 20_

Ex.mos Senhores
Fonseca & Ca.
Porto

Ex.mos Senhores

Venho acusar a receção da v/ estimada carta de 17 do mês findo, na qual V. Ex.as se queixam da demora na entrega das mercadorias encomendadas em 11 de agosto.

Não foi por culpa nossa que elas não foram expedidas, mas devido à greve dos trabalhadores da doca, que durou uns 15 dias. Logo que seja possível informarei por *e-mail* a data do embarque.

Lamentando a inconveniência que esta demora lhes cause, somos com estima e consideração.

De V. Ex.as
Atenciosamente

Assinatura

11

(3)

Com os melhores cumprimentos; Com estima e consideração, subscrevo-me
Best regards, Yours sincerely, Yours faithfully

De V. Ex.ᵃˢ	In Brazil:	**V.S.as**
Atenciosamente	*or*	**Atentamente**
Yours faithfully		Yours faithfully

Commercial letter in reply to a complaint

Lisbon, May 8, 20_

Messrs Fonseca & Co.
Porto

Dear sirs,

I acknowledge receipt of your [esteemed] letter of the 17th of last month, in which you complained about the delay in the delivery of the goods you ordered on August 11.

It was not through any fault of our own that they were not shipped but due to a strike by dockworkers, which lasted 15 days. As soon as it is possible, I will inform you by email of the shipment date.

We very much regret the inconvenience this delay may have caused you and send our esteem and consideration.

Yours faithfully,

Signature

11

Week

■ *idiomatic expressions with the verbs* **dar, deixar, estar, fazer, ficar, ir, pôr, querer,** *and* **ser**
■ *Portuguese equivalents of some English idioms*
■ *useful words and phrases for specific situations*

EXPRESSIONS LINKED TO CERTAIN VERBS

dar

dar horas to strike the hour
dar corda ao relógio to wind a clock/watch
dar baixa ao hospital to be admitted to the hospital
O médico deu-lhe alta. The doctor discharged him/her (from the hospital). (see also **ter**)
A janela dá para o mar. The window looks out on the sea.
dar para to have a flair for, to be enough for
Ela dá para a música. She has a flair for music.
Este peixe não dá para todos. This fish is not enough for everyone.
dar por to notice
O polícia não deu por isso. The police didn't notice it/ weren't aware of it/didn't realize it.
dar com to come across, to bump into (someone)
Dei com o Carlos no cinema. I bumped into Carlos in the movie theater.
dar-se bem/mal em… to be well and happy/unhappy in … (a place)
Dou-me muito bem no Algarve. The Algarve suits me (the climate, etc.).
dar-se bem/mal com… to get along well/badly with …
Dou-me muito mal com ela. I don't get along with her.
dar em nada to come to nothing
Ele deu em louco. He became mad/crazy.
dar à luz to give birth
dar por certo to take for granted
Quem me dera! How I wish! Would that I might!
  (pretérito mais-que-perfeito of **dar)**
  ao Deus dará aimlessly (left to one's own fate)
  dar uma vista de olhos to take a quick look at/through

deixar

Ele deixou de fumar. He stopped smoking.
Deixe-me em paz. Leave me alone.
Ela deixou as cartas para outro dia. She put off (writing) the letters until another day.
Elas deixaram as camas por fazer. They left the beds unmade.

estar

estar para sair to be at the point of going out
O teatro estava às moscas. The theater was empty (literally "to the flies").
O cinema estava à pinha. The movie was packed.
O trabalho está por fazer. The work remains undone.
A gasolina está pela hora da morte. Gasoline has become very expensive.
estar de boa maré/má maré to be in a good mood/ bad mood
estar em dia com ... to be up to date with ...
estar com fome/sede (in Brazil: **sêde**) to be hungry/thirsty
estar com sono/frio/calor to be sleepy/cold/hot
estar com sorte/ciúmes/medo (in Brazil: **mêdo**) to be lucky/jealous/afraid
estar com pressa/vontade de/razão to be in a hurry/to feel like/to be right
um mal-estar indisposition, discomfort, embarrassment

fazer

fazer a barba to shave ("the beard")
fazer anos to have one's birthday
Ele faz trinta anos hoje. He is thirty today.
Faz bom/mau tempo. The weather is good/bad.
Ela só faz asneiras. She only makes mistakes.
Você fez muito bem/mal. You did the right/wrong thing.
Nadar faz bem à saúde. Swimming is good for health.

12

fazer as vontades de ... to do the will of/to give in to
  the wishes of someone
Farei o possível. I will do my best.
Que é feito dela? What has happened to her?
fazer-se de bobo to play dumb
fazer uma viagem to take a trip/to go on a journey

ficar

Este chapéu fica-lhe bem. This hat suits you.
Ele ficou bem no exame. He passed the exam.
Fica para a semana. Let's make it next week.
Fica para a outra vez. We'll make it another time.
Fique descansado/a. Don't worry./Rest assured.
Fico contente. I am so happy. (regarding good news)
Isto fica entre nós. This is between us.
Ele ficou sem dinheiro. He was left without money.

ir

ir ter com to go to meet
ir de encontro a to collide with
ir de avião/de autocarro (in Brazil: **omnibus**)/**de barco**
  to fly/to go by bus/boat
ir a pé/a cavalo to walk, to go on foot/to ride
Vai mal de saúde. He is in poor health.
  (also: **Está muito mal.**)
Como vão? How are you (pl.)?
Ir a Roma e não ver o Papa. To go to Rome and not
  see the Pope. (i.e., to go to a place and not see what it's
  famous for or not to accomplish one's mission)
Ela vai aos ares. She hits the ceiling/blows up in a rage.
Vamos! Let's go!
Sempre foi a Portugal? Did you go to Portugal
  (in the end/after all)?

12

pôr

pôr a mesa to set/lay the table
pôr de castigo to punish
Ela pô-lo na rua. She kicked him out.
  (literally "put him in the street")
pôr-se a to begin to
Ela pôs-se a falar muito depressa. She began to
  speak hurriedly.
O homem põe e Deus dispõe. Man proposes and
  God disposes.
sem tirar nem pôr precisely/just like that
o pôr do sol sunset

querer

se quiser if you like
como quiser (queira) as you wish
sem querer unintentionally
Ela fez por querer. She did it on purpose.
Queira sentar-se. Please sit down.
Quem quer vai, quem não quer manda. If you want
  a thing done, do it yourself.

ser

É isso mesmo. That's just it.
É sempre assim. It always happens that way.
Como foi que...? How did it happen that ...?
É por minha conta. It's on me. (i.e., I'll pay the bill.)
a não ser que unless
se eu fosse você/a ti... if I were you . . .
Seja como for... Be that as it may ...
tal como deve ser as it should be
É a minha vez. It's my turn.
o ser humano human being

12

PORTUGUESE EQUIVALENTS OF SOME ENGLISH IDIOMS

What's it about? **De que se trata?**
Say no more about it. **Não fale mais nisso.**
Forget about it. **Não pense mais nisso.**
ages ago **há muito tempo**
all at once **de repente**
all the better **tanto melhor**
It's all the same to me. **É-me indiferente. / Tanto se me dá.**
as it were/so to speak **por assim dizer**
as you like **como quiser**
to back out (of an agreement) **faltar ao prometido**
Stop beating around the bush. **Deixe-se de rodeios.**
I hope you'll get better soon. **Desejo-lhe/-te as melhoras.**
By the way ... **A propósito...**
How did it happen? **Como aconteceu isso?**
Come on!/Come along!/Let's go! **Vamos!**
to be at ease **pôr-se/estar à vontade**
Take it easy. **Não se canse./Não te canses.**
to fall asleep **adormecer**
to fall in love **apaixonar-se**
to get dark **escurecer/anoitecer**
It's getting late. **Está a fazer-se tarde.**
  (in Brazil: **entardecendo**)
to get fired/dismissed **ser despedido**
Get out! **Fora! / Rua!**
How's life?/How are things? **Como lhe/te corre a
  vida?/Como vão as coisas?**
I couldn't get a word in edgewise. **Não consegui abrir
  a boca./Não abri bico.**
I give in. **Desisto./Dou-me por vencido.**
I give up. **Desisto.**
I'm going to get ready. **Vou-me arranjar./Vou-me
  aprontar.**
going like hot cakes **vendendo-se muito bem**
He is hard up. **Ele está em apuros/sem dinheiro.**
I work hard. **Trabalho muito.**
hard to please **difícil de contentar**
He has hardly said a word. **Ele mal disse uma palavra.**
Help! **Socorro!**

12

Can't be helped! **Não há remédio!/Que remédio!**
Help yourself! **Sirva-se!/Serve-te!**
a long way off **a uma grande distancia**
So long! **Adeus!/Até logo!**
to look after **tomar conta de/olhar por**
to look like **parecer-se com**
to make a mistake **enganar-se**
to make the most of it **tirar o melhor partido**
to make up one's mind **decidir-se a**
It doesn't matter./Never mind. **Não faz mal./**
  Não tem importância.
Do you mind? **Importa-se?/Importas-te?**
Watch the step! **Cuidado com o degrau!**
Mind your own business. **Meta-se/Mete-te na sua/tua**
  vida./Isto não tem nada que ver consigo/contigo.
to be in a good frame of mind/in a good mood **estar**
  bem-disposto
She doesn't mince words. **Ela não tem papas na língua.**
more or less **mais ou menos**
to the right **à direita**
to be right **ter razão**
It's all right. **Está bem.**
You have no right. **Não tem/tens o direito.**
right and wrong **o bem e o mal**
It serves you right! **É bem feito!**
You don't say!/Don't tell me! **Não me diga/digas!**
to be out of one's senses **perder o juízo**
to drive out of his/her senses **fazer perder a cabeça a...**
It doesn't make any sense. **Não faz sentido nenhum.**
so so **assim-assim**
to take advantage of/to take the opportunity
  aproveitar-se de
to take (unfair) advantage of **tirar partido de/abusar**
to take a photograph **tirar uma fotografia**
to take place **realizar-se/efetuar-se**
It takes all the fun out of it. **Tira-lhe a graça toda.**
Where there's a will, there's a way. **Querer é poder.**
That's up to you. **Isso é consigo/contigo.**
against my will **contra minha vontade**
If God wills it. **Se Deus quiser.**
It isn't worth it. **Não vale a pena.**

12

More useful words & phrases

em viagem traveling

Há uma demora/um atraso de duas horas.
There's a delay of two hours.
O avião está atrasado. The plane is late.
devido ao nevoeiro/greve due to fog/strike
**Onde é a alfândega/a saída/o Posto de Primeiros
Socorros?** Where is Customs/the exit/the First Aid
station? (in Brazil: **o Posto de Pronto-Socorro**)
Tem alguma coisa a declarar? Do you have anything
to declare?
Falta-me uma mala. One of my suitcases is missing.
o cinto de segurança safety belt
É proibido fumar. Smoking is not allowed.
Sinto-me enjoado/a. I feel airsick/seasick.
Onde são os lavabos/é o toilete/é a retrete?
Where are the restrooms?
A que horas atracou o barco?
What time did the boat arrive?
Os passageiros já estão a desembarcar.
The passengers are already disembarking.
As passagens são caras.
The fares (by boat or plane) are expensive.
o bagageiro porter

no comboio on the train

Quero dois bilhetes de ida e volta para o Porto.
I'd like two return tickets to Porto.
É preciso marcar os lugares?
Is it necessary to book the seats?
De que linha parte o comboio (rápido) para …
From which platform does the (fast) train leave for …
(in Brazil: train = **trem**)
É direto ou tenho de mudar (in Brazil: **… de
trocar**)**?** Is it direct, or do I have to change?
o vagão-restaurante dining car
o vagão-cama (in Brazil: **vagão-dormitório**) sleeping car
a sala de espera waiting room
o carregador porter

12

o depósito de bagagens lost luggage office
O comboio vem as horas (in Brazil: **... no horário certo)/atrasado/adiantado?** Will the train be on time/late/early?
a estação de caminho de ferro railway station

de carro by car

a autoestrada motorway, highway
a estrada nacional national road, interstate
a passagem de nível level crossing, railroad crossing
a passagem de peões/passadeira pedestrian crossing
o sentido único one way
o perigo danger
o desvio diversion, detour
a curva perigosa dangerous bend
o estacionamento proibido no parking
trabalhos/obras (in Brazil: **trabalhadores**) road work
a estação de serviço service station
a bomba de gasolina gas pump
Mostre-me a sua carta de condução (in Brazil: **carteira de motorista/carta de direção**).
Show me your driver's license.
a matrícula registration number

as avarias car problems ("breakdowns")

Rebentou-me um pneu. I have a flat tire.
A bateria está descarregada. The battery is dead.
afinar os travões (in Brazil: **acertar os freios**) to adjust the brakes
Preciso de ar nos pneus. I need air in the tires.
uma lata de óleo a can of oil
água no radiador water in the radiator
os faróis headlights
o tubo de escape exhaust pipe
as velas spark plugs
as mudanças gears
a caixa de velocidades transmission

12

a embraiagem clutch
o para-brisas windshield
o limpa-para-brisas wipers
a roda sobresselente spare tire
marcha-atrás (in Brazil: **marcha a ré**) reverse
ponto-morto neutral

os acidentes accidents

ferido/morto injured/dead
Mande chamar o médico. Send for the doctor.
Desmaiou./Está a sangrar. He/she has fainted./
   He/she is bleeding.
A ambulância já vem. The ambulance is on its way.
Embateu em.../Chocou com...
   It hit .../It crashed against ...
a camioneta truck, bus
a bicicleta bicycle
Tentava ultrapassar o outro. He/she was trying to
   overtake the other.
Ia a grande velocidade. He/she was going at
   high speed.
O carro derrapou. The car skidded.
a rua escorregadiça/escorregadia slippery road
testemunhas witnesses (m. & f.)
Ouvi o barulho. I heard the noise.
Onde fica a esquadra/o posto de polícia?
   Where is the police station?

no consultório médico at the doctor's

Estou constipado (in Brazil: **resfriado**). I have a cold.
O senhor está com a gripe. You (m.) have the flu.
a receita/os remédios prescription/medicine
**Tenho dores de cabeça/das costas/da garganta/
   da barriga.** I have a headache/backache/sore throat/
   stomachache.
a insolação sunstroke
a intoxicação alimentar food poisoning

a enxaqueca migraine
a febre/fraco fever/weak
Desloquei o braço/o tornozelo. I sprained my
arm/my ankle.
Deite-se./Dispa-se./Vista-se.
Lie down./Get undressed./Get dressed.
a injeção/o xarope/os comprimidos/a pomada
injection/cough syrup/tablets/ointment
dar entrada no hospital to go into hospital
Teve alta do hospital. He/she was discharged
from hospital.
Estimo as melhoras. I hope you'll get better soon.
o/a enfermeiro/a nurse
a prisão de ventre constipation
a tontura/os arrepios de frio dizziness/shivers

o/a dentista dentist

as dores de dentes toothache
Abra a boca. Open your mouth.
Vou tirar uma radiografia. I'm going to take an X-ray.
Precisa de arrancar este dente. You need to have this
tooth pulled out.
Este dente precisa de ser chumbado. This tooth
needs to be filled.
Tem uma cárie. You have a cavity.
Quanto é a consulta? How much is the consultation
fee?
Está a doer-me/magoar-me. You are hurting me.

no hotel at the hotel

A que horas é o pequeno-almoço (in Brazil: **café
da manhã**)**?** What time is breakfast (served)?
O horário das refeições está no seu quarto.
The list of mealtimes is in your room.
Pode acordar-me às sete horas?
Can you wake me up at seven?
pensão completa/meia-pensão full board/half-board

12

só dormida room only
o quarto de casal com casa de banho (in Brazil: **com banheiro**) double room with bathroom
o quarto para pessoa só com chuveiro single room with shower
Tem Wi-Fi? Do you have Wi-Fi?
Qual é a palavra-passe? What's the password?
Tem aqui facilidades para enviarmos um *e-mail*?
Are there any facilities here for us to send an email?
Preciso de uma outra almofada/cobertor.
I need another pillow/blanket.
Como se acende/apaga a televisão/a luz?
How do you switch on/off the TV/the light?
Onde se pode alugar um automóvel?
Where can I rent a car?
O ar condicionado/aquecimento central está avariado.
The air-conditioning/central heating is not working.
Como se abrem os estores?
How do you work these blinds?
O serviço e o imposto estão incluídos?
Does that include all services and taxes?
Onde fica a piscina? Where is the swimming pool?
Tenho uma reclamação/queixa a fazer.
I have a complaint to make.
Onde está o gerente? Where is the manager?
Gostei da estada. I enjoyed my stay.
É muito amável. You are very kind.
Obrigado/a pela sua ajuda. Thank you for your help.

no restaurante in the restaurant

Traga-me a ementa/a conta. Bring me the menu/bill.
a garrafa de vinho tinto/branco bottle of red/white wine
o pão com manteiga/compota bread and butter/jam
a torrada toast
O que me recomenda/aconselha?
What do you recommend?
Tem algo vegetariano/vegan?
Do you have anything vegetarian/vegan?
Não como carne/peixe. I don't eat meat/fish.

12

É orgânico? Is it organic?
o prato do dia dish of the day
malpassado/bem passado/picante
  rare/well-done/spicy
Preciso de sal/pimenta/mostarda.
  I need salt/pepper/mustard.
Não tenho guardanapo. I don't have a napkin.
Esqueceu-se da salada. You have forgotten the salad.
o jarro de água jug of water
Este copo está sujo. This glass is dirty.
Falta uma faca/uma colher/um garfo.
  A knife/spoon/fork is missing.
A refeição estava ótima/excelente.
  The meal was super/excellent.
a gorjeta tip
Fique com o troco. Keep the change.
Não quero mais. Basta./Chega. I don't want
  any more. I've had enough.
um pouco mais a little more

as casas e situações domésticas house and household
situations

o anúncio advertisement
venda/compra/renda
  sale/purchase/rent
senhorio/a/inquilino/a/notário/a
  landlord/tenant/attorney
a escritura/a câmara deeds/town hall
a contribuição predial/a camarária
  municipality rates/local tax
as casas assoalhadas/divisões rooms (not counting
  kitchen, bathroom)
Já dei o sinal. I have already paid the deposit.
Ela vai mudar-se. She is going to move (house).
o orçamento/as despesas estimate (budget)/expenses
O autoclismo não funciona. The flush is not working.
A torneira da banheira/do lavatório está a pingar.
  The faucet of the bath/sink is dripping.
Os canos estão entupidos. The pipes are blocked.

12

O/a empregado/a doméstico/a hoje fez gazeta.
Today the cleaner has not come.
passar a ferro/engomar to iron
lavar a louça/a roupa to wash the dishes/clothes
O frigorífico/Esta mesa está sujo/a. The refrigerator/
This table is dirty.
Tem muitas nódoas. It has many stains.
A campainha da porta não toca.
The doorbell doesn't ring.
o quarto/a sala de visitas/a cozinha
bedroom/living room/kitchen
a casa de jantar/a casa de banho/a varanda
dining room/bathroom/balcony
O leite está azedo. The milk has gone sour.
As maçãs estão podres. The apples are rotten.
Há falta de batatas. There aren't enough potatoes.
Vou descascar estas laranjas. I'm going to peel
these oranges.

as compras em geral shopping (in general)

a drogaria pharmacy
a mercearia grocery
o mercado market
Quero dois pacotes de... I want two packages of ...
De que marca? Which brand?
Quanto custa? How much is it?
a caixa/carteira de fósforos box/book of matches
os lenços de papel tissues, kleenex
os postais ilustrados/a revista/o jornal
postcards/magazine/newspaper
Tem um carregador de telemóvel?
Do you have a phone charger?
o posto dos correios/os selos/via aérea
post office/stamps/by airmail
Onde se levantam as encomendas postais?
Where does one collect registered mail?

12

a roupa ou o vestuário e as cores clothes and colors

a sapataria shoe store
Qual é o tamanho/o número que calça/que veste?
What size do you wear in shoes/clothes?
Estes sapatos não me servem.
These shoes don't fit me.
o salto alto/baixo/raso high/low/flat heel
o departamento de roupa desportiva/infantil
sportswear/children's department
o tecido/a seda (in Brazil: **sêda**)**/o algodão/a lã**
cloth/silk/cotton/wool
Este casaco (in Brazil: **paletó**) **está-me apertado.**
This coat is tight on me.
Esta cor (in Brazil: **côr**) **não me fica bem.**
This color does not suit me.
o fato (in Brazil: **terno**)**/a saia/o casaco**
suit/skirt/coat (jacket)
o vestido/as calças/os calções (in Brazil: **calças de esporte**) dress/trousers/shorts
o fato de banho (in Brazil: **maiô de banho**) swimsuit
o sobretudo/a camisola/a blusa
overcoat/jumper/blouse
o impermeável/o guarda-chuva/o cinto/as luvas
raincoat/umbrella/belt/gloves
as meias/as cuecas/o sutiã stockings/underpants/bra
as peúgas/a camisa de noite (in Brazil: **camisola**)**/
a roupa interior** socks/nightgown/underwear
a gravata/o pijama/o colete/a camisa
tie/pajamas/vest/shirt
verde/azul/branco/preto/encarnado/roxo
green/blue/white/black/red/purple
vermelho/amarelo dark red/yellow
cinzento/castanho (in Brazil: **marron**)**/cor-de-rosa**
gray/brown/pink
cor de laranja/claro/escuro/dourado
orange/light/dark/gold
prateado/bege/cor de camelo/creme
silver/beige/camel colored/cream
Esta saia precisa de ser limpa a seco.
This skirt needs to be dry cleaned.

12

o/a cabeleireiro/a, o barbeiro hairdresser, barber

Quero madeixas. I want highlights.
um penteado simples/elegante a simple/elegant hairstyle
um corte/só aparado/ripado (in Brazil: **desfiado/a**
  unhas feitas) a cut/just trimmed/backcombed
Deixe-o comprido/curto. Leave it long/short.
Tenho o cabelo encaracolado/ondulado/liso.
  I have curly/wavy/straight hair.
Não quero o cabelo frisado. I don't want my hair frizzy.
Quanto tempo preciso de esperar?
  How long do I need to wait?
Quero arranjar as unhas. I want my nails done.
Quero só fazer a barba. I just want a shave.
Não toque no bigode. Don't touch the moustache.
Faça o risco ao lado/ao meio. Part it on the side/center.

os divertimentos e desportos (in Brazil: **esportes**)
entertainment and sports

ir a um concerto/ir ver uma peça de teatro/
  ir ao cinema go to a concert/play/film
o jogo de futebol (in Brazil also: **partida de futebol**)/
  o empate soccer match/draw
a bilheteira/lotação esgotada (in Brazil: **bilheteria/**
  ingressos esgotados) ticket office/sold out
ir à discoteca go clubbing
andar a cavalo to ride (a horse)
ir andar de bicicleta/fazer caminhada em montanha
  go cycling/go hiking
jogar às cartas/o xadrez to play cards/chess
o barco à vela/a motor/remar sailing/boating/to row
a natação swimming
esquiar/fazer esqui to ski
ir surfar/praticar surf go surfing
a caça submarina scuba diving
o corte/recinto de ténis (in Brazil: **quadra de tênis**)
  tennis court
o campo de golfe golf course

12

Appendix – verbs

Regular, stem-changing, and irregular verbs, and verbs requiring a preposition

REGULAR VERBS
[only the conjugation endings are given]

INDICATIVE MOOD

Present tense			Preterite			Imperfect		
-ar	**-er**	**-ir**	**-ar**	**-er**	**-ir**	**-ar**	**-er**	**-ir**
-o	-o	-o	-ei	-i	-i	-ava	-ia	-ia
-as	-es	-es	-aste	-este	-iste	-avas	-ias	-ias
-a	-e	-e	-ou	-eu	-iu	-ava	-ia	-ia
-amos	-emos	-imos	-ámos	-emos	-imos	-ávamos	-íamos	-íamos
-am	-em	-em	-aram	-eram	-iram	-avam	-iam	-iam

Future*			Conditional*			Past participle		
-ar	**-er**	**-ir**	**-ar**	**-er**	**-ir**	**-ar**	**-er**	**-ir**
-ei	-ei	-ei	-ia	-ia	-ia	-ado	-ido	-ido
-ás	-ás	-ás	-ias	-ias	-ias	(used in compound		
-á	-á	-á	-ia	-ia	-ia	tenses, such as the		
-emos	-emos	-emos	-íamos	-íamos	-íamos	perfect tenses, etc.)		
-ão	-ão	-ão	-iam	-iam	-iam			

SUBJUNCTIVE MOOD

Present			Imperfect			Future**		
-ar	**-er**	**-ir**	**-ar**	**-er**	**-ir**	**-ar**	**-er**	**-ir**
-e	-a	-a	-asse	-esse	-isse	-ar	-er	-ir
-es	-as	-as	-asses	-esses	-isses	-ares	-eres	-ires
-e	-a	-a	-asse	-esse	-isse	-ar	-er	-ir
-emos	-amos	-amos	-ássemos	-êssemos	-íssemos	-armos	-ermos	-irmos
-em	-am	-am	-assem	-essem	-issem	-arem	-erem	-irem

Imperative				Present participle		
-ar	**-er**	**-ir**		**-ar**	**-er**	**-ir**
-a	-e	-e	(you, familiar)	-ando	-endo	-indo
-e	-a	-a	(you, formal)			
-emos	-amos	-amos	(let us . . .)			
-em	-am	-am	(you, plural)			

NOTES:
* When forming the future and conditional, the endings in the previous table are added to the infinitive form of the verb: e.g., **falar → falarei, falaria**. In other tenses, the conjugated endings are added just to the stem (i.e., without ir, ar, er): **falo, falei**, etc.

** The personal infinitive of regular verbs (see section 10.1 for more) is formed in the same way as the future subjunctive.

STEM-CHANGING VERBS

In these verbs, the stem of the infinitive changes in the first-person singular of the present tense indicative and consequently in all persons of the subjunctive.

e to **i**

Infinitive	Present tense	Present subjunctive
seguir (to follow)	**sigo**	**siga, -as, -a, -amos, -am**
preferir (to prefer)	**prefiro**	**prefira,** etc.
mentir (to lie)	**minto**	**minta,** etc.
vestir (to dress)	**visto**	**vista,** etc.
servir (to serve)	**sirvo**	**sirva,** etc.
sentir (to feel)	**sinto**	**sinta,** etc.
divertir-se (to enjoy)	**divirto-me**	**me divirta,** etc.
despir (to undress)	**dispo**	**dispa,** etc.
conseguir (to succeed, manage, achieve)	**consigo**	**consiga,** etc.
repetir (to repeat)	**repito**	**repita,** etc.

o to **u**

cobrir (to cover)	**cubro**	**cubra,** etc.
descobrir (to discover)	**descubro**	**descubra,** etc.
dormir (to sleep)	**durmo**	**durma,** etc.
tossir (to cough)	**tusso**	**tussa,** etc.

Certain verbs, such as **subir** ("to climb," "to go up"), **fugir** ("to run away," "to flee"), **destruir** ("to destroy"), and **construir** ("to build"), have a different type of stem change, as in the following example in the present indicative.

eu subo	nós subimos
tu sobes	eles/elas sobem
ele/ela sobe	

Other stem-changing verbs that alter only in the first-person singular present tense and the subjunctive:

perder (to lose)	perco	perca, etc.
medir (to measure)	meço	meça, etc.
valer (to be worth)	valho	valha, etc.
pedir (to ask for)	peço	peça, etc.
ouvir (to hear, listen)	ouço	ouça, etc.

VERBS WITH A SPELLING CHANGE

In certain verbs, the last consonant of the stem is modified or changed in certain persons and tenses in order to preserve the original pronunciation of the infinitive. The most common examples are as follows:

-car→ -qu before e or i
brincar (to play) brinquei (I played)

-çar→ -c before e or i
começar (to begin) comecei (I began)

-cer→ -ç before a, o, or u
conhecer (to know) conheço (I know)

-gar→ -gu before e or i
chegar (to arrive)→ cheguei (I arrived)

-ger, -gir→ j before a, o, or u
fugir (to flee) fujo (I flee)

-guer, -guir→ g before a, o, or u
perseguir (to pursue) persigo (I pursue)

IRREGULAR VERBS

In order to make it easier to remember these irregular conjugations, they are listed by similarity where applicable. Only the first-person singular is given for tenses (imperfect, future, etc.) in which the verb conjugates following the pattern for regular verbs.

dar	estar	ser	ir
to give	to be	to be	to go

Present tense

dou	estou	sou	vou
dás	estás	és	vais
dá	está	é	vai
damos	estamos	somos	vamos
dão	estão	são	vão

Preterite

dei	estive	fui	fui
deste	estiveste	foste	foste
deu	esteve	foi	foi
demos	estivemos	fomos	fomos
deram	estiveram	foram	foram

Imperfect

dava	estava	era	ia

Future

darei	estarei	serei	irei

Conditional

daria	estaria	seria	iria

Present subjunctive

dê	esteja	seja	vá
dês	estejas	sejas	vás
dê	esteja	seja	vá
dêmos	estejamos	sejamos	vamos
deem	estejam	sejam	vão

Imperfect subjunctive

desse	estivesse	fosse	fosse

Future subjunctive

der	estiver	for	for

Personal infinitive

dar	estar	ser	ir
dares	estares	seres	ires
dar	estar	ser	ir
darmos	estarmos	sermos	irmos
darem	estarem	serem	irem

Imperative

dá	está	sê	vai
dê	esteja	seja	vá
dêmos	estejamos	sejamos	vamos
deem	estejam	sejam	vão

Past participle

dado	estado	sido	ido

Present participle

dando	estando	sendo	indo

ter	vir	ver	pôr
to have	to come	to see	to put

Present tense

tenho	venho	vejo	ponho
tens	vens	vês	pões
tem	vem	vê	põe
temos	vimos	vemos	pomos
têm	vêm	veem	põem

Preterite

tive	vim	vi	pus
tiveste	vieste	viste	puseste
teve	veio	viu	pôs
tivemos	viemos	vimos	pusemos
tiveram	vieram	viram	puseram

Imperfect

tinha	vinha	via	punha

Future

terei	virei	verei	porei

Conditional

teria	viria	veria	poria

Present subjunctive

tenha	venha	veja	ponha

Imperfect subjunctive

tivesse	viesse	visse	pusesse

Future subjunctive

tiver	vier	vir	puser

Personal infinitive

ter	vir	ver	pôr

Imperative

tem	vem	vê	põe
tenha	venha	veja	ponha
tenhamos	venhamos	vejamos	ponhamos
tenham	venham	vejam	ponham

Past participle

tido	vindo	visto	posto

Present participle

tendo	vindo	vendo	pondo

trazer	dizer	fazer	saber	haver	poder
to bring	to say	to do	to know	to have	to be able to

Present tense

trago	digo	faço	sei	hei	posso
trazes	dizes	fazes	sabes	hás	podes
traz	diz	faz	sabe	há	pode
trazemos	dizemos	fazemos	sabemos	havemos	podemos
trazem	dizem	fazem	sabem	hão	podem

Preterite

trouxe	disse	fiz	soube	houve	pude
trouxeste	disseste	fizeste	soubeste	houveste	pudeste
trouxe	disse	fez	soube	houve	pôde
trouxemos	dissemos	fizemos	soubemos	houvemos	pudemos
trouxeram	disseram	fizeram	souberam	houveram	puderam

Imperfect

trazia	dizia	fazia	sabia	havia	podia

Future

trarei	direi	farei	(regular)	(regular)	(regular)
trarás	dirás	farás			
trará	dirá	fará			
traremos	diremos	faremos			
trarão	dirão	farão			

Conditional

traria	diria	faria	(regular)	(regular)	(regular)
trarias	dirias	farias			
traria	diria	faria			
traríamos	diríamos	faríamos			
trariam	diriam	fariam			

Present subjunctive

traga	diga	faça	saiba		possa
tragas	digas	faças	saibas		possas
traga	diga	faça	saiba	haja	possa
tragamos	digamos	façamos	saibamos		possamos
tragam	digam	façam	saibam		possam

Imperfect subjunctive

trouxesse	dissesse	fizesse	soubesse	houvesse	pudesse

Future subjunctive

trouxer	disser	fizer	souber	houver	puder

Personal infinitive

trazer	dizer	fazer	saber	haver	poder

Past participle

trazido	dito	feito	sabido	havido	podido

Present participle

trazendo	dizendo	fazendo	sabendo	havendo	podendo

Imperative

traz(e)	diz(e)	faz(e)	sabe		pode
traga	diga	faça	saiba	haja	possa
tragamos	digamos	façamos	saibamos		possamos
tragam	digam	façam	saibam		possam

ler	crer	querer	rir*	caber
to read	to think, believe	to want	to laugh	to fit in, be contained

Present tense

leio	creio	quero	rio	caibo
lês	crês	queres	ris	(otherwise
lê	crê	quer(e)	ri	conjugates
lemos	cremos	queremos	rimos	like **saber** in
leem	creem	querem	riem	all tenses)

Preterite

li	cri	quis	ri
leste	creste	quiseste	riste
leu	creu	quis	riu
lemos	cremos	quisemos	rimos
leram	creram	quiseram	riram

Imperfect

| lia | cria | queria | ria |

Future

| lerei | crerei | quererei | rirei |

Conditional

| leria | creria | quereria | riria |

Present subjunctive

| leia | creia | queira | ria |

Imperfect subjunctive

| lesse | cresse | quisesse | risse |

Future subjunctive

| ler | crer | quiser | rir |

Personal infinitive

| ler | crer | querer | rir |

Past participle

| lido | crido | querido | rido |

Present participle

| lendo | crendo | querendo | rindo |

Imperative

lê	crê	quer(e)	ri
leia	creia	queira	ria
leiamos	creiamos	queiramos	riamos
leiam	creiam	queiram	riam

* **sorrir** ("to smile") conjugates like **rir**.

SOME REMARKS

1 The **pretérito mais-que-perfeito** (or pluperfect) is seldom used in speech but may be encountered in writing. In speech, the past perfect (**tinha falado**) is preferred.

To conjugate the pluperfect, **-ara, -era, -ira** is added to the stem of the infinitive: e.g., **falara, comera, partira** (first- and third-person sing.). In irregular verbs, the endings are added to the stem of the preterite or future subjunctive: e.g., **dissera, fizera, fora, dera, trouxera, vira, tivera**.

2 The subjunctive mood can also be used to form perfect tenses: the present perfect subjunctive (e.g., **tenha falado**), the past perfect subjunctive (e.g., **tivesse falado**), and the future perfect subjunctive (e.g., **tiver falado**).

3 The auxiliary verb **haver** sometimes replaces the verb **ter** in perfect tenses, especially in literary works. This is usually the only time you will come across it fully conjugated.

Typically, **haver** is used as an impersonal verb and so is only conjugated in the third-person singular in all tenses, e.g., **há**, which means "there is"/"there are," etc.

SOME VERBS THAT REQUIRE A PREPOSITION BEFORE THE INFINITIVE OF ANOTHER VERB

acabar de to finish (doing something)
Acabo de comer.
I have just eaten/finished eating.

acabar por to end up (doing ...)
Ele acabou por consentir.

aconselhar a to advise
Aconselho-o a ver o médico.

ajudar a to help
Ela ajuda-me a lavar a louça.

começar a to begin
Ele começou a falar.

começar por to begin by
Ele começou por dizer.

esquecer-se de to forget
Esqueci-me de te dizer que...

gostar de to like
Gosto de comer.
(with this verb, a preposition is also needed before a noun)

lembrar-se de to remember
Não me lembro do seu nome.

obrigar a to force, compel
Obriguei-a a dizer a verdade.

pedir para to ask (to)
Pedi-lhe para fazer isso.

pensar em to think of
Pensei em falar contigo.

precisar de to need
Preciso de falar com ele.
(prep. also needed before a noun)

voltar a to do something again
Voltei a vê-lo.

voltar para to return (in order to do something)
Voltei para te ver.

SOME VERBS FOLLOWED BY A PREPOSITION

acreditar em to believe
Acredito em ti.

aproximar-se de to go near
Aproximei-me dele.

assistir a to attend
Assisti a uma tourada.

casar-se com to get married
Ela casou-se com um inglês.

chegar a to arrive at
Cheguei à conclusão. Cheguei a Faro.

dar com to come across, to bump into
Dei com a Manuela no armazém.

dar para to overlook
O meu quarto dá para o jardim.

dar para to be enough for
Esta carne dá para cinco pessoas.

dar por to notice
Não dei por ela.

duvidar de to doubt	**Duvido da sua palavra.**
encontrar-se com to meet (by arrangement, mostly)	**Vou-me encontrar com eles.**
ir a, ir para to go to (**ir a** implies a shorter stay than **ir para**)	**Vou a Paris em negócios.**
olhar para to look at	**Ele olhou para mim.**
parecer-se com to look like, resemble	**Ela parece-se com o pai.**
pegar em to pick up (in Brazil: **pegar** without preposition)	**Ele pegou na mala.**
queixar-se de to complain about	**Eu queixei-me da comida.**
reparar em to notice	**Reparei no teu vestido.**
sonhar com to dream of	**Sonhei contigo.**
sorrir para to smile at	**Ela sorriu para a menina.**
vir a, vir para to come (**vir a** implies a shorter stay than **vir para**)	**Ele veio a Londres.**

Key to exercises

Exercise 1: 1 A rapariga. 2 O rapaz. 3 O escritório.
4 A casa. 5 As flores. 6 Os empregos. 7 Os gatos.
8 As alunas. 9 A mesa. 10 As mesas.

Exercise 2: 1 Uma viagem. 2 Um escritório.
3 Um avião. 4 Uma cidade. 5 Um bilhete.
6 Uns homens. 7 Umas mulheres. 8 Umas
viagens. 9 Uns escritórios. 10 Umas raparigas.

Exercise 3: 1 I have. 2 Do you have? (polite)
3 We don't have. 4 You have (pl.). 5 Does she
have? 6 You do not have (pl. formal). 7 Don't
they have? 8 (Eu) Não tenho dinheiro.
9 A senhora tem um bilhete? 10 Eles têm bons
empregos. 11 Vocês têm uma casa? 12 Tu tens
um escritório. 13 (Nós) Temos fome. 14 Não há
uma mesa. 15 Há quanto tempo fala inglês?

Practice exercise: 1 Não. A senhora Smith é
inglesa. 2 Ela agora mora em Lisboa. 3 Sim, tem
um bom emprego. 4 Não, como auditora de uma
grande empresa. 5 Ela tem um escritório no
Estoril. 6 O marido dela é professor de inglês.
7 Não. A Maria Helena é do Algarve. 8 Ela é
médica. 9 Não. Lisboa é a capital de Portugal.
10 Sim, Lisboa é uma cidade linda.

WEEK 2

Exercise 1: 1 Sou inglesa. 2 O senhor é o gerente deste hotel? 3 Ele é aborrecido. 4 Ela é uma secretária. 5 Isto é muito importante. 6 Nós somos amigas. 7 Eles são velhos. 8 São estas as malas? 9 These suitcases are not mine. 10 This is impossible. 11 I'm not a secretary, I'm a teacher. 12 We are friends. 13 Are you (pl.) married? 14 Are they tourists?

Exercise 2: 1 Estou em Londres. 2 Tu estás cansada? 3 Ela não está em casa. 4 Estamos a trabalhar todos os dias. 5 Eles estão enganados. 6 O comboio (in Brazil: trem) está atrasado. 7 Estou aborrecida. 8 I am eating. 9 Are you at home today? 10 We are not mistaken. 11 You (sing. formal) are hungry. 12 They are looking beautiful. 13 The young women are ready. 14 Today I am not in the office.

Exercise 3: 1 O livro está na mesa. 2 A mulher esta à porta. 3 Ela vai pelo parque. 4 O escritório do tio Tomás. 5 Estou ao telefone. 6 A água está no copo. 7 Estou aqui em férias. 8 We are going to the market. 9 I am going home. 10 She is in the bathroom. 11 In a situation like this. 12 He came in through the window. 13 I am speaking of the accident. 14 He gave the money to the young man.

WEEK 3

Exercise 1: 1 We are looking for a house.
2 They don't speak Portuguese very well, but
they understand everything. 3 She never accepts
my invitation. 4 What (will) you (formal) have?
5 He opens/is opening the window. 6 I study
every day. 7 You (pl.) don't eat much. 8 I am
leaving at 9 o'clock. 9 You (formal pl.) work a
lot. 10 Are you (formal pl.) buying the tickets?

Exercise 2: 1 O meu irmão procura um emprego
em Moçambique. 2 Ele aprende português.
3 Precisa de ajuda? 4 Aceito o seu convite com
prazer. 5 Comem e bebem demasiado.
6 O comboio parte a horas. (in Brazil: O trem
parte no horário certo.) 7 Ele vende o carro.
8 Hoje não compro nada. 9 A minha irmã não
come à uma hora. 10 Ela está de dieta.

Exercise 3: 1 Which is the nearest station from
here? 2 What is your address? 3 She never does
what I want. 4 Why don't you go by car?
5 I believe it is very far. 6 How is business
going? 7 I don't know whom I should pay.
8 Onde vai? 9 Quanto devo? 10 Não me disse o
seu nome. 11 Que disse (você)? 12 Quem é
aquele homem lindo? 13 Quando vai a França?
14 As chaves que ela me deu não são minhas.

Exercise 4: 1 That shop on the corner. 2 We are going to that beach. 3 What is this? 4 This is a computer. 5 Please shut that door. 6 This is my husband and that is my son. 7 These keys are not mine. 8 Esta casa é grande. 9 O que é isso? 10 Não quero aqueles livros ali. 11 Isto é impossível. 12 Ele está naquele hotel. 13 Esta mala é daquele homem. 14 Os bilhetes estão nesta mala (de senhora).

Practice exercise: dizia-me; há; perto; dois minutos daqui; por aqui; a direito; passar; vê logo; ir ao; fica; um pouco; melhor; apanhar; está ali; esquerda; virar; esquina; sabem; fica; Claro; conhecem; a palma da mão.

WEEK 4

Exercise 1: 1 I like your house very much.
2 This is your glass and that one (over there) is
his. 3 Your daughter is very nice. 4 Our holidays
begin in June. 5 My wife always arrives late.
6 Go and wash your hands. 7 We are going to
their house. 8 São estas as suas malas? 9 O meu
telefone está sempre avariado. 10 Isto não é
meu. 11 Não sei o nome deles. 12 A vossa casa é
muito longe. 13 A nossa filha chega amanhã.
14 O amigo dele é americano.

Exercise 2: 1 I finish work at six o'clock.
2 We're going to spend two weeks at the
beach. 3 She has four brothers (or brothers
and sisters). 4 The book costs 15 euros.
5 This elevator only takes five people. 6 I go to
Paris every four weeks. 7 My birthday is on
September 20. 8 Ele começa o trabalho às oito
horas. 9 Ela tem dois meninos e três meninas.
10 Eu escrevo à minha mãe de cinco em cinco
dias. 11 Ele parte a vinte de maio (or Ele parte
no dia vinte de maio). 12 Ele não trabalha há dez
dias. 13 Tenho trinta e cinco anos. 14 São seis
menos um quarto.

Exercise 3: 1 Next week I'm going to my aunt's (house). 2 Last month my brother went to work in Brazil. 3 My sons (or children) will arrive in 15 days' time. 4 Tonight we are going to the theater. 5 Spring is my favorite season. 6 Yesterday it was very cold. 7 The day after tomorrow we will have the results of our examinations. 8 Vou passar o Natal com os meus amigos em Lisboa. 9 Este ano não tenho férias. 10 Ela vai passar o verão no Algarve. 11 Ontem esteve (fez) calor. 12 Faço anos no domingo. 13 Amanhã de manhã começo o trabalho (começo a trabalhar). 14 Julho, agosto e setembro são meses muito quentes em Portugal.

Exercise 1: 1 Hoje o tempo está mau. 2 Ela é uma boa atleta. 3 Não sei onde está o meu mapa francês. 4 A minha irmã é mais velha do que eu. 5 A minha amiga é espanhola, mas o marido dela é inglês. 6 É uma boa coisa que (você) faz. 7 Há muitas pessoas simpáticas neste mundo (or Há muita gente simpática neste mundo). 8 O meu colega está muito contente no Brasil. 9 É uma instituição europeia. 10 A mãe da minha amiga é (uma) poetisa. 11 Tenho um grande carro verde. 12 O meu primo é um bom escritor e a mulher dele é também uma boa escritora. 13 O António é um jornalista português. 14 Esta galinha está crua.

Exercise 2: 1 Duas salas. 2 Os meus irmãos. 3 As flores são lindas. 4 Estes problemas são difíceis. 5 No verão, há muita gente nas praias. 6 Três estudantes ingleses. 7 Quatro lençóis. 8 Os meus amigos são muito amáveis. 9 Não conheço estes homens. 10 As crianças alemãs não gostam de cães. 11 Compro cinco pães todos os dias. 12 Ela gosta de todos os animais. 13 A minha irmã tem olhos azuis. 14 Tenho as mãos sujas. 15 Estes limões são bons. 16 Os meus pais estão sempre tão felizes/contentes.

Exercise 3: 1 Yesterday I received a letter from my friend. 2 We liked your home very much.
3 Last week we visited a very modern school.
4 They have left for Brazil. 5 Have you sold your house yet (already)? 6 No, we haven't sold our house yet. 7 They haven't written yet.
8 Não compreendi. 9 Que beberam eles?
10 Já comi. 11 Quando partiram eles? 12 A que horas partiu o comboio? 13 Não abrimos a janela. 14 Ele não comeu ontem à noite.
15 Você falou com a sua mãe? 16 Conheci o seu irmão em Lisboa.

Exercise 4: 1 Come here. 2 Speak slowly. 3 Don't make a noise. 4 Go that way. 5 Don't be silly.
6 Be still. 7 Bring the wine list. 8 Fale devagar.
9 Abramos a janela. 10 Fechem a porta. 11 Não comam tão depressa. 12 Vejamos … 13 Venham já. 14 Vamos! 15 Não falem tão alto. 16 Não diga nada.

WEEK 6

Exercise 1: 1 When I was a child I used to learn everything more easily. 2 Before I used to eat a lot, but not now. 3 We used to go to the beach every day. 4 Yesterday we went to the countryside. 5 It was underneath this tree that I used to sit. 6 What were you doing? 7 I was taking a bath. 8 A que horas tomou o seu pequeno-almoço? 9 Dizia-me, por favor, onde é (fica) a paragem do autocarro (in Brazil: a parada do ônibus)? 10 Sabes tocar guitarra? 11 Chovia a cântaros/potes quando saímos. 12 Ele ouvia enquanto eu falava. 13 Já comia. 14 Ontem (à noite) jantei com a minha sogra.

Exercise 2: 1 The plane took six hours to get there. 2 Today I don't want to play with the children; I prefer to play chess. 3 He comes here a lot. 4 She went to New York, and from there she went to Mexico. 5 Doctor, how many tablets do I have to take? 6 I had to take out (withdraw) money from my bank account. 7 Como está o tempo aí? 8 As suas/tuas luvas estão por aí. 9 A paragem do autocarro (in Brazil: A parada do ônibus) fica (está) ali. 10 Cá estou (Aqui estou)! 11 Vejo um barco acolá. 12 As suas/tuas chaves estão aqui.

Exercise 3: 1 Give him/her my regards. 2 She rang me up last night. 3 He/she saw him last week. 4 I don't know them well. 5 They visit us every year. 6 We want to see him. 7 I'm going to help you/her. 8 You (pl.) help him very much. 9 He does not want the apples, but I'm going to give them to him. 10 You live near me. 11 I won't eat without you. 12 Come with me now to have coffee, and afterward I'll come with you to the hairdresser. 13 The dogs are with us, but the cats are with them (f.). 14 Who told you that?

Exercise 4: 1 Mostre-nos o que encontrou (achou). 2 Vai procurá-la. (in Brazil: Vá buscar a ela.) 3 Estas flores são para mim? 4 Antes que me esqueça tenho de lhes dizer... 5 Ele esperou por nós. 6 Venha comigo. 7 Não há segredos entre nós. 8 Conto contigo. 9 Ele não mo emprestou. 10 Eles ajudam-no. 11 A minha mãe não me telefonou. 12 Não preciso dele. 13 Chamei-o, mas ele não me ouviu. 14 Vi-os a semana passada. 15 Ele vai vê-la.

Exercise 1: 1 Do you want (to have) tea or coffee? 2 I don't want either tea or coffee. I prefer orange juice. 3 I'll either go to the movies or stay at home and watch television, I'm not sure yet. 4 I've never seen such a well-organized exhibition. 5 He has no scruples at all. 6 I'll never again buy electrical appliances secondhand. 7 You have nothing to do with it. (It's none of your business.) 8 No one speaks English here. 9 I don't know anything. 10 We didn't go anywhere.

Exercise 2: 1 Já comeste bacalhau à Gomes de Sá? 2 Ninguém me disse isso. 3 Já que estou aqui, envio este *e-mail* também. 4 Nunca o vimos. 5 Não tenho nenhuma. 6 Ainda não vi este filme. 7 Ela já não gosta dele. 8 Ele já traz a ficha. 9 Já que ela pediu desculpa, considero o assunto encerrado/considero que o assunto está encerrado/considero que o assunto acabou. 10 Elas nunca foram a lado nenhum.

Exercise 3: 1 Alguém aqui fala inglês? 2 O senhor pediu-me uma colher ou uma faca? 3 Nem uma nem outra, pedi-lhe um garfo. 4 Ele tem algumas esperanças. 5 Cada qual tem o seu gosto. 6 Está tudo caríssimo. 7 Têm algumas revistas inglesas? 8 São ambos escritores. 9 O jantar estava péssimo. 10 A minha tia está muito mal. 11 Ele é o homem mais rico do mundo. 12 Tenho boas notícias para ti. 13 Ela está tão feliz como eu. 14 Camões foi o maior poeta português.

Exercise 4: 1 Quando lhe escreverá? (or Quando lhe vai escrever?) 2 Ele tem de trabalhar muito. 3 Não o tomaremos. 4 Começarei a minha história. 5 Quem ganhará? 6 Chegaremos no próximo mês. 7 Seria a verdade? 8 I would say he is lying. 9 I won't forget you. 10 I would do everything for her. 11 They will give him/her/ you my new address. 12 I will go to Japan. 13 I have to go to the dentist. 14 Will it be very expensive?

WEEK 8

Exercise 1: 1 She had already studied Portuguese when she was a child. 2 This year there have been many plane accidents. 3 The woman was already dead when the doctor arrived.
4 The tables were already set, but the guests had not arrived yet. 5 I had never seen so many people in my life. 6 She was expelled from school. 7 It is said (They say) that the firm (Messrs) Agiota & Co. is going bankrupt.
8 One must not deceive (cheat, mislead) others.
9 They had not washed themselves yet.
10 The weather has been very bad.

Exercise 2: 1 They felt (were) disappointed.
2 I got up very early. 3 He never remembers my birthday. 4 She got dressed in a hurry.
5 He smells awful because he never washes himself. 6 How do you say "table" in Portuguese? 7 They looked at each other.
8 Serve yourself while the food is hot.
9 We don't know each other. 10 I complained to the police. 11 Go away. 12 It's sunny.
13 I forgot about him. 14 English newspapers are sold here.

Exercise 3: 1 Lembro-me dele. 2 Não me sentia bem. 3 Queixámo-nos da comida. 4 Tem chovido muito este ano. 5 Já tinha posto a carta no correio. 6 Bebe-se muito vinho em Portugal, mas os portugueses não se embriagam com frequência. 7 A janela estava aberta. 8 A lotaria foi ganha por uma mulher pobre. 9 A minha saia estava rota. 10 Foram todos presos. 11 Eles olharam-se um ao outro. 12 Não tenho viajado este ano. 13 Ouve-se muita música inglesa em Portugal. 14 Não quero servir-me. 15 Vimo-nos por acaso. 16 Aqui vendem-se jornais.

Exercise 1: 1 It is necessary for them to study hard. (They must study hard.) 2 Hopefully they won't come in late. 3 Perhaps (Maybe) I will go out tomorrow. 4 I want you to do that at once. 5 Tell him not to come in until I call him. 6 I hope your wife is better. 7 I don't think he is a good soccer player. 8 We want a man who has the courage of his convictions. 9 Whether I like it or not, I have to attend the meeting tomorrow. 10 Diga-lhe que não vá à reunião. 11 Embora eu não fale português muito bem, compreendo tudo. 12 Quer que lhe traga a lista dos vinhos? 13 É melhor que eu vá agora. 14 Não creio que haja jornais hoje. 15 Eles têm pena (Lamentam) que não possa vir esta noite. 16 Por favor, não faça (nenhum) barulho.

Exercise 2: 1 It was a pity (a shame) he could not come. 2 I wanted you (pl.) to learn Portuguese as quickly as possible. 3 I didn't see any house that pleased me (that I liked). 4 Perhaps he had already left. 5 If it were not so expensive, we would buy a farm in the Algarve. 6 We did not want you (pl.) to bring presents. 7 I don't know whether it is raining. 8 If it rains I'll take an umbrella. 9 Until the factory workers go back to (resume) work, we cannot increase production. 10 Come to our house whenever you want. 11 As soon as you get a job in Mozambique, let me know (tell me). 12 Do what you can. 13 Invite (pl.) whom you wish. 14 Whoever wants to come with me should come.

Exercise 3: 1 Assim que puderes, telefona-me, por favor. 2 Se ele não fosse tão preguiçoso (mandrião), não teria perdido esse emprego. 3 Foi preciso que eles chamassem a polícia. (Foi preciso chamarem a polícia.) 4 Disse-lhes para se irem embora. (Disse-lhes que se fossem embora.) 5 Diga o que disser, eu não acredito que ela seja desonesta. 6 Quando me reformar, escreverei muitos livros. 7 Faça como quiser. (Faça o que quiser.) 8 Aconteça o que acontecer, e apesar do tempo (clima), sempre amarei a Inglaterra. 9 Não havia ninguém que falasse inglês. 10 Enquanto estiverem em minha casa, são meus convidados. 11 Lamentei que não pudessem vir. (Lamentei não poderem vir.) 12 Se (você) perdeu esta oportunidade, foi porque quis. 13 Embora protestassem (tivessem protestado) muitas vezes, a situação continuou a ser a mesma. 14 Talvez ela tenha dito a verdade.

Note: The alternatives given above demonstrate the use of the personal infinitive, which is explained in week 10.

Exercise 1: 1 This book is for us to read. 2 I don't want to buy the car unless you agree (without you agreeing). 3 It's a shame (pity) you cannot come next Sunday. 4 It was good that you brought your coats, because it's going to be cold. 5 I fear they are cross with me. 6 They didn't come because they were tired. 7 It was impossible for us to go to the bullfight. 8 You? Winning the World Cup? (doubt and mild derision implied) 9 Eles vão partir antes de chegarmos. 10 Foi impossível vermos o ministro. 11 Surpreende-me tu dizeres uma coisa dessas. (Surpreende-me que tu digas uma …) 12 Disse-lhes adeus antes de partirem (… antes de eles partirem). 13 Não posso dar uma opinião até sabermos tudo. (… até que saibamos tudo / … enquanto não soubermos tudo). 14 Não almoçámos por não termos tempo (… porque não tivemos tempo).

Exercise 2: 1 I have no time to write letters.
2 (Mrs.) Amelia is going to the doctor on Wednesday. 3 My sister is going into the hospital on Tuesday for an operation on her throat.
4 I am telling you this for your own good.
5 I didn't mean to hurt him. (It was not intentional that I hurt him.) 6 Last month I went to Paris to visit my aunt. 7 Thank you for your kindness. 8 As far as I'm concerned (Personally), I don't mind. 9 Não tenho nenhumas notícias (novidades) para ti. 10 Ele lutou pelos direitos do ser humano. 11 Ele foi a Londres em negócios. 12 O senhor vai para casa agora?
13 O António foi trabalhar para a África.
14 Peço desculpa (Desculpe-me) por chegar atrasada/o. 15 Vou para a cama.

Practice exercise: sinto-me; escrito; foi; parece; conspirado; tenha; tido; começaram; era; vais; estão; está; sei; chovido; sofreram; deve; causado; lembro; comi; chovido; estou; pudéssemos; estaríamos; ficariam; Agradeço; irmos; são; creio; vai; aceitámos; fez; passarmos; assistirmos; queremos; possas; forem; podermos; haja; mataria; diz-; conseguirei; dão; prometendo; recordo.

Mini-dictionary

Although the following is not an exhaustive list of words found in the course, it should be helpful as a quick reference. Reference numbers after certain entries indicate sections where more information is given. See sections 4.2–4.3 and 4.5–4.7 for the numbers, days of the week, months, seasons, etc.

a, an um, uma
able capaz;
  to be able to poder
abolish abolir
about acerca de
  to be about to estar para
above acima (de)
abroad no estrangeiro (m.)
accept aceitar
accident acidente (m.)
address morada (f.), endereço (m.),
  direção (f.)
  to address (someone) dirigir-se a
admire admirar; **admired**
  admirado/a
advertise pôr um anúncio
advertisement anúncio (m.)
after depois de
afternoon tarde (f.)
against contra
age idade (f.)
agree concordar, estar de acordo
all todo/a/s
allow permitir, deixar
almost quase
alone só, sozinho/a
already já
also também
always sempre
American americano/a
among entre
and e
angry zangado/a
  to be angry/cross
  zangar-se com
animal animal (m.)
announce anunciar

announcement anúncio (m.)
any nenhum/nenhuns (m.),
  nenhuma/as (f.),
  qualquer, quaisquer
anyone ninguém, qualquer
  pessoa
anything nada, qualquer coisa
apartment andar (m.)
appear aparecer
apple maçã (f.)
arrival chegada (f.)
arrive chegar
as como, tão
as much/many tanto/a/s
  as much as possible tanto
  quanto possível
as soon as assim que
  as soon as possible tão depressa
ask (to inquire) perguntar
ask for pedir
assist ajudar
at (section 2.6)
at least pelo menos
at once já, imediatamente
attend assistir a
aunt tia
awful terrível, péssimo/a

bad mau, má
badly mal
bank banco (m.)
banker banqueiro/a
bankruptcy falência (f.)
  to go bankrupt falir
bath banho (m.)
bathtub banheira (f.)

bathroom casa (f.)/quarto (m.) de banho, banheiro (m.) (Br.)
be ser, estar (section 2.1–2.3)
beach praia (f.)
bear (animal) urso (m.)
bear (v.) aguentar, suportar
beautiful lindo/a, belo/a
bed cama (f.), leito (m.)
bedroom quarto (m.) (de dormir)
beer cerveja (f.)
before antes de, perante
begin começar, principiar
behind atrás de
believe crer em, acreditar em
beside ao lado de
besides além de
better melhor
between entre
big grande
bill conta (f.)
birthday aniversário (m.)
  to have one's birthday fazer anos
black preto, negro
blue azul
boat barco (m.)
book livro (m.)
book (v.) marcar, reservar
boring/bored aborrecido/a
borrow pedir emprestado
both ambos/as
  both he and I tanto eu como ele
bottle garrafa (f.)
box caixa (f.), caixote (m.)
boy menino (before puberty), rapaz (after puberty)
bread pão (m.)
break (v.) quebrar, partir
breakdown (car) avaria (f.); **(nervous)** esgotamento (m.) nervoso
breakfast pequeno-almoço (m.), café da manhã (m.) (Br.)
bring trazer
brother irmão
brother-in-law cunhado

brown castanho, marron (Br.)
brush (n.) escova (f.), pincel (m.)
bull touro, toiro (m.)
bullfight tourada (f.)
bus autocarro (m.), ônibus (m.) (Br.), machimbombo (m.) (Mozambique)
business negócio, negócios (m.)
but mas
buy comprar
by por, através

call (v.) chamar;
  to be called chamar-se
can (to be able to) poder
car carro (m.), automóvel (m.)
care cuidado/a
  careless descuidado/a
carriage camioneta (f.), carruagem (f.)
carry levar
cat gato/a
certainly certamente, claro, com certeza
chance oportunidade (f.)
  by chance por acaso
change mudança (f.); (v.) mudar, trocar
cheap barato/a
cheat (v.) enganar, fazer batota
check (v.) verificar
cheese queijo (m.)
chicken galinha (f.) (hen), frango (m.) (food & male chicken)
child/children criança/as (f.)
choice escolha (f.)
choose escolher
Christmas Natal (m.)
Christmas Eve Consoada (f.)
church igreja (f.)
cigarettes cigarros (m.)
cigars charutos (m.)
citizen cidadão / cidadã
city cidade (f.)
climb (v.) subir, trepar
clock relógio (m.)
coat casaco (m.), paletó (m.) (Br.)

coffee café (m.)
cold frio/a
come vir
  come back voltar
  come in entrar
complain queixar-se
complaint queixa (f.)
computer computador (m.);
  (laptop) computador portátil
contents conteúdo (m.)
continue continuar
cost custo (m.); (v.) custar
count (v.) contar
country país (m.)
  countryside campo (m.)
courage coragem (f.)
course curso (m.)
(of) course com certeza
cousin primo/a
cover (v.) cobrir
cross cruz (f.); (v.) atravessar
  to be cross estar zangado/a,
  zangar-se
cup chávena (f.), xícara (f.)
customer cliente (m. & f.),
  freguês/freguesa
customs costumes (m.),
  alfândega (f.)
customs officer funcionário/a
  da alfândega

damage prejuízo (m.), dano (m.)
dark escuro/a
darling querido/a
daughter filha
day dia (m.)
dead morto/a
decide decidir
dentist dentista (m. & f.)
die morrer, falecer
diet dieta (f.)
difficult difícil
dinner jantar (m.)
  to dine jantar
dirty sujo/a
disappear desaparecer

disappointed desanimado/a,
  desiludido/a, desapontado/a
dishonest desonesto/a
do (v.) fazer
doctor doutor/doutora, médico/a
dollar dólar (m.)
door porta (f.)
down (not working) em baixo
downstairs em baixo, lá/cá em
  baixo
dream sonho (m.); (v.) sonhar
dress vestido (m.)
  to get dressed vestir-se
drink bebida (f.); (v.) beber
drive conduzir, guiar
drought seca (f.)
drunk bêbado/a, embriagado/a
  to get drunk embriagar-se
dye (v.) tingir

each cada
  each one cada cual
  each other um ao outro/
  uma à outra
ear orelha (f.), ouvido (m.)
early cedo
easy fácil
  easily facilmente
eat comer
either ou
employee empregado/a,
  funcionário/a
employment emprego (m.)
English inglês/inglesa
enjoy divertir-se, gozar
enough bastante
enter entrar
equally igualmente
evening tarde (f.), noite (f.),
  tardinha (f.)
every cada
every day todos os dias
everyone toda a gente,
  todo o mundo (Br.)
everything tudo
exam exame (m.)

examine examinar
example exemplo (m.)
except exceto
exercise exercício (m.)
exhibition exposição (f.)
expect esperar, contar com
expenses despesas (f.)
expensive caro/a
explain explicar
eye olho (m.)

fall (v.) cair
far longe, distante
farm quinta (f.)
fast depressa, adiantado/a
father pai
  father-in-law sogro
fault culpa (f.)
favor favor (m.)
fear medo (m.); (v.) ter medo,
  temer, recear
feel (v.) sentir, sentir-se
fetch buscar, ir buscar
few alguns/algumas, poucos/as
fight (v.) lutar
fill encher
  fill in preencher
find achar
finish (v.) acabar, terminar
fire fogo (m.), incêndio(m.),
  lume (m.)
flight voo (m.)
floor chão (m.), soalho (m.);
  andar (storey) (m.)
flower flor (f.)
fog nevoeiro (m.)
follow seguir
foot pé (m.)
for (sections 2.6, 10.4)
foreign estrangeiro/a
forget esquecer, esquecer-se de
fork garfo (m.)
fortnight quinzena (f.), quinze dias
fortunately felizmente
freeze gelar, congelar
French francês/francesa

friend amigo/a
from de
fruit fruta (f.)
full cheio/a, pleno/a
furniture mobília (f.)
  pieces of furniture móveis (m.)

garden jardim (m.)
general geral;
  (army) general
gentleman cavalheiro, senhor
German alemão/alemã
get obter, arranjar
get up levantar-se
girl menina (before puberty),
  rapariga, moça (after puberty)
give dar
glass vidro (m.), copo (m.), taça (f.)
go ir, ir-se embora
  go out sair
gold ouro, oiro (m.)
good bom/boa
  goodness bondade (f.)
goodbye adeus
goods mercadoria (f.), géneros (m.)
grape uva (f.)
gray cinzento
great (important) grande
green verde
grow crescer
guess (v.) adivinhar
guest convidado/a

hair cabelo (m.)
half metade, meio/a
hand mão (f.)
happen acontecer
happy feliz
hardly mal
hat chapéu (m.)
have ter (section 1.4)
hazard azar (m.)
head cabeça (f.)
health saúde (f.)
healthy saudável
hear ouvir

heavy pesado/a
height altura (f.)
help ajuda (f.), socorro (m.);
  (v.) ajudar
  help yourself sirva-se (polite),
  serve-te (fam.)
here aqui, cá
high alto/a
holidays férias (f.)
home casa (f.), lar (m.)
hope esperança (f.); (v.) esperar
horse cavalo (m.)
host anfitrião/anfitriã
hot quente, calor
hotel hotel (m.)
hour hora (f.)
house casa (f.)
how como (section 3.2)
however contudo
humanity humanidade (f.)
humankind homem (m.), os
  homens, o ser humano
hunger fome (f.)
hurry pressa (f.)
hurt (v.) magoar, ferir
husband marido, esposo

if se
ill doente
immediately imediatamente
important importante
impossible impossível
in em
increase aumento (m.);
  (v.) aumentar
information informação (f.)
intend tencionar
introduce apresentar
invitation convite (m.)
invite (v.) convidar
Italian italiano/a

Japan Japão
  Japanese japonês/japonesa
job emprego (m.), trabalho (m.)
journey viagem (f.)

juice sumo (m.), suco (m.) (Br.)
keep (v.) guardar, manter
key chave (f.)
kind amável;
  kindness amabilidade (f.)
king rei
  kingdom reinado (m.)
knife faca (f.)
know (be acquainted with)
  conhecer
  know (how or a fact) saber
knowledge sabedoria (f.),
  conhecimento (m.)

lady senhora
lamp candeeiro (m.), lâmpada (f.)
large grande
last último/a
late tarde, atrasado/a
laugh (v.) rir
  laughter riso (m.)
law lei (f.), direito (m.)
lawyer advogado/a
lazy mandrião / mandriona,
  preguiçoso/a
learn aprender
leave (v.) partir, sair;
  (leave something) deixar
lemon limão (m.)
lend emprestar
less menos
lesson aula (f.), lição (f.)
let (rent) alugar;
  (allow) deixar
letter carta (f.)
lie mentira (f.)
  to tell a lie mentir
lie down deitar-se
lift elevador (m.); (v.) levantar,
  elevar; **(get a ride in a car)** boleia
  (f.), carona (f.)(Br.)
light luz (f.); (v.) acender;
  (color) claro
like como, semelhante
like (v.) gostar de
  Lisbon Lisboa

listen ouvir, escutar
little pequeno/a, pouco/a
live (v.) viver
  to live at morar
living room sala (f.) de estar/de
  visitas
loan empréstimo (m.)
London Londres
long longo/a, comprido/a
long for (v.) ter saudades de
  longing saudade/s (f.)
look (v.) olhar
  look for procurar, buscar (Br.)
lose perder
loss prejuízo, perda
loud alto/a
love (v.) amar, gostar de
love (n.) amor (m.)
low baixo/a
luck sorte (f.)
  bad luck azar (m.), má sorte
luggage malas (f.), bagagem (f.)
lukewarm morno/a
lunch almoço (m.)

magazine revista (f.)
mail correio (m.); (v.) pôr no
  correio
majority maioria (f.),
  maioridade (f.)
make (v.) fazer
  made feito
man homem
manager gerente (m. & f.)
many muitos/as
market mercado (m.), praça (f.)
married casado/a
  to get married casar-se
me/mine (section 6.5)
meat carne (f.)
meet encontrar, encontrar-se com
meeting encontro (m.), reunião (f.)
memories memórias (f.),
  recordações (f.)
message recado (m.),
  mensagem (f.)

milk leite (m.)
mind cérebro (m.), mente (m.)
mind (v.) importar-se
miss (the train, etc.) perder;
  miss (someone/something)
  ter saudade(s) de
mistake erro (m.)
  to be mistaken estar enganado
  (section 2.4)
money dinheiro (m.)
month mês (m.)
more mais
moreover além disso, tanto
  mais que
morning manhã (f.)
most mais, a maior parte de,
  máximo
mother mãe
  mother-in-law sogra
move (v.) mover, transportar,
  mexer-se, comover;
  move house mudar-se
much muito
music música (f.)
must dever
my (section 6.5)

naked nu/nua
name nome (m.)
near perto de
nearly quase
necessary preciso/a, necessário/a
need (v.) precisar de
neighbor vizinho/a
neither nem
nephew sobrinho
never nunca, jamais
new novo/a
news notícias (f.), novidades (f.)
newspaper jornal (m.)
next próximo/a, a seguir
nice simpático/a
niece sobrinha
night noite (f.)
no, not não
noise barulho (m.)

no one ninguém
nor nem
nothing nada
notice aviso (m.), comunicado (m.);
  (v.) notar
now agora
number número (m.)

obey obedecer
of de
office escritório (m.)
officer funcionário/a;
  (police) polícia
often muitas vezes, frequentemente
on em
once uma vez;
  at once já, imediatamente
only só, somente, apenas
open (v.) abrir
operation operação (f.)
opinion opinião (f.)
opportunity oportunidade (f.)
or ou
orange laranja (f.)
order encomenda (f.);
  (v.) encomendar, mandar,
  mandar vir
organize organizar
other outro/a;
  otherwise senão
ought dever
our, ours nosso/a/s (section 4.1)
out fora
owe dever

page página (f.)
painter pintor/pintora
paper papel (m.)
parcel embrulho (m.), pacote (m.)
park parque (m.)
part parte (f.)
partner sócio/a, parceiro/a
pay (v.) pagar
pea ervilha (f.)
pear pera (f.)
pen caneta (f.)

pencil lápis (m.)
people gente (f.), pessoas (f.)
pepper pimenta (f.)
perhaps talvez
permit autorização (f.), licença (f.)
person pessoa (f.)
photograph fotografia (f.)
pick up (v.) apanhar
picture quadro (m.), gravura (f.)
pin alfinete (m.)
pink cor-de-rosa
pipe cano (m.);
  (smoking) cachimbo (m.)
pity pena (f.), lástima (f.)
plane avião (m.)
plate prato (m.)
play (v.) brincar, jogar, tocar
  (section 6.2)
pleasant agradável
please por favor, faz favor,
  faça o favor; (v.) agradar
pleasure prazer (m.), gosto (m.)
pocket algibeira (f.), bolso (m.)
police polícia (f.)
poor pobre
Portuguese português/portuguesa
possible possível
post correio (m.);
  postman/woman carteiro/a
poverty pobreza (f.)
prefer preferir
present (gift) presente (m.)
prevent evitar, impedir
price preço (m.)
print (v.) imprimir
promise prometer
proof prova (f.)
protest (v.) protestar
prove provar
purchase compra, compras (f.)
purple roxo
put (v.) pôr
  put in meter

quarter quarto (m.)
queen rainha

question pergunta (f.), questão (f.)
quickly depressa
quiet calado/a

rabbit coelho (m.)
race corrida (f.)
railways caminho de ferro (m.),
  ferrovias (m.)
rain chuva (f.); (v.) chover
rare raro/a
  (steak) malpassado
raw cru/crua
read ler
ready pronto/a
receive receber
recommend recomendar
red encarnado
refuse (v.) recusar, recusar-se
regards cumprimentos (m.)
remain ficar, continuar
remember lembrar-se de
repeat (v.) repetir
reply resposta (f.); (v.) responder
resolve (v.) resolver, decidir-se a
respect (v.) respeitar
rest resto (m.), descanso (m.);
  (v.) descansar
result resultado (m.)
resume recomeçar, retomar
retire reformar-se, aposentar-se;
  afastar-se
return (v.) voltar, regressar
rich rico/a;
  richness riqueza (f.)
right (direction) direito/a;
  (correct) certo/a
  to be right ter razão
ring (v.) tocar, telefonar
river rio (m.)
room quarto (m.), sala (f.), casa (f.)
run (v.) correr

sad triste
safe (strongbox) cofre (m.)
  (to be) safe seguro/a, salvo/a,
  livre

salary ordenado (m.), salário (m.)
salt sal (m.)
same mesmo
sample amostra (f.)
satisfy satisfazer
say dizer
scarcely apenas, mal
(on) schedule a tempo,
  a horas
school escola (f.)
scruples escrúpulos (m.)
sea mar (m.)
season estação (f.)
seat lugar (m.), assento (m.)
secret segredo (m.)
secretary secretário/a
see ver
seem parecer
send mandar, enviar
serious sério/a, grave
several vários/as
shame vergonha (f.)
sheet lençol (m.)
ship barco (m.), navio (m.)
shoe sapato (m.)
shop loja (f.)
short curto/a;
  in short em suma;
  shortly em breve
shortage falta (f.)
show espetáculo (m.); (v.) mostrar
shut (v.) fechar, encerrar
silly tonto/a, parvo/a
silver prata (f.)
sing cantar
sir senhor
sister irmã
sit down sentar-se
situation situação (f.)
skirt saia (f.)
sleep (v.) dormir;
  to be sleepy ter sono
slow lento/a, devagar
slowly devagar, lentamente
small pequeno/a
smell cheiro (m.), aroma (f.)

smile (v.) sorrir
smoke (v.) fumar
so assim, portanto; tão
soccer futebol (m.)
some algum/a/s (section 7.4)
something alguma coisa
sometimes às vezes
son filho
  son-in-law genro
soon em breve
  as soon as assim que, logo que
sorry desculpe
  to be sorry ter pena, pedir
  desculpa
Spain Espanha
  Spanish espanhol/espanhola
speak falar
spend gastar
spoon colher (f.)
stamp selo (m.)
start (v.) começar, principiar
station estação (f.)
stay (v.) ficar
still ainda
story história (f.), conto (m.)
street rua (f.)
strength força (f.)
strike greve (f.)
strong forte
student aluno/a,
  estudante (m. & f.)
study estudo (m.), (v.) estudar
sugar açúcar (m.)
suit fato (m.), terno (m.) (Br.)
suitcase mala (f.)
sun/sunshine sol (m.)
supply (v.) fornecer
sure (to be) ter a certeza
swim (v.) nadar
swimming pool piscina (f.)

table mesa (f.)
take tomar, levar, tirar
tall alto/a
tea chá (m.)
teach ensinar

teacher professor/professora
telephone telefone (m.);
  (call) telefonema (m.),
  chamada (f.); **(cell phone)**
  telemóvel (m.), celular (m.) (Br.)
television televisão (f.)
tell dizer, contar
than que, do que
thank (v.) agradecer;
  thank you obrigado/a
that (sections 3.2–3.3)
the (section 1.2)
theater teatro (m.)
then então
there ali, acolá, lá, aí
there is/are há
therefore portanto
these, this, those
  (section 3.3)
thing coisa (f.)
think pensar, crer, achar
thirst sede (f.)
throat garganta (f.)
throw (v.) atirar
thunder trovoada (f.)
thus assim
ticket bilhete (m.)
time tempo (m.) (general), vez (f.)
  (occasion), hora (f.) (of day),
  vagar (m.) (leisure)
tired cansado/a
to a, para
today hoje
together juntos/as
too também
  too much demasiado, de mais
tool ferramenta (f.)
touch (v.) tocar, apalpar,
  mexer em
town cidade (f.)
train comboio (m.), trem (m.) (Br.)
travel (v.) viajar
traveler viajante (m. & f.)
trip volta (f.), giro (m.), pequena
  excursão (f.), viagem (f.);
  (v.) tropeçar

true verdade, verdadeiro/a
truth verdade (f.)
try tentar, provar, experimentar
turn (v.) voltar, virar

ugly feio/a
umbrella guarda-chuva (m.),
  sombrinha (f.), para-sol (m.)
uncle tio
underneath debaixo de, sob,
  debaixo
understand perceber,
  compreender, entender
understanding compreensão (f.),
  entendimento (m.)
unfortunately infelizmente
until até
upstairs em cima, lá em cima
useful útil

very muito
village aldeia (f.), povoação (f.)
visa visto (m.)
visit visita (f.); (v.) visitar

wait (v.) esperar
  waiting espera (f.), à espera,
  esperando
waiter empregado/a
walk (v.) andar a pé,
  caminhar, passear;
  (n.) passeio (m.)
want (v.) querer, desejar
warm quente (m.), calor (m.)
wash (v.) lavar,
  (oneself) lavar-se
watch relógio (m.); (v.) vigiar
water água (f.)
way (route) caminho (m.);
  (manner) jeito (m.)
we/us etc. (sections 2.4, 6.5)
weak fraco/a
weather tempo (m.)
week semana (f.)
weight peso (m.)
well (adv.) bem; (n.) poço (m.)

what/when/where/which
  (section 3.2)
whether se
white branco
who/whose/whom (section 3.2)
whole todo, inteiro
why porque, porquê
wife esposa, mulher
win (v.) ganhar
wind vento (m.)
  windy ventoso
window janela (f.)
wine vinho (m.)
winter inverno (m.)
wish desejo (m.); (v.) desejar
with com
without sem
woman mulher
word palavra (f.)
work trabalho (m.); (v.) trabalhar
worker operário/a,
  trabalhador/trabalhadora
world mundo (m.)
worried preocupado/a,
  apoquentado/a, inquietado/a,
  aflito/a
worry (v.) preocupar-se,
  apoquentar-se
worse pior
worth valor (m.)
  to be worth ter o valor de,
  ser digno de
wound ferida (f.); (v.) ferir
write escrever
writer escritor/escritora
written escrito/a

year ano (m.)
yearly anual, por ano, anualmente
yellow amarelo
yes sim
yesterday ontem
yet ainda, no entanto, contudo
you/yours etc. (sections 1.8, 4.1)
young jovem
youth juventude (f.)

Index

The numbers refer to sections, not pages.